MONEY
MINDFULNESS
DAILY

What School Failed To Teach You

The Secrets To Earning The
Money You Deserve

Ed J C Smith

Wednesday – 25th April Thur
2nd May

Aspire

ISBN 978-1-9996456-0-1

First published by Ed J C Smith

This book is dedicated to **YOU**.

To give you the answers that you have been searching for.

No matter how dark it gets, the light is never too far away.

A Quick Thank You For Your Investment

Thank you for taking the time to read this book. It is my pleasure to spend time with you and to have the opportunity to help you in this vital area of your life. I trust that you have invested in this book with a desire to create daily mindfulness around your money. You may want to create more wealth and better financial results. You may dream about having more time, freedom and balance so that you can truly live the life you want, on your terms. You may want to start or grow your own business, or you may want to improve your current position and job prospects.

My Personal Promise To You And What You Will Get From Reading This Book

What you invest into your life, is what you will get out. So, if you don't have the results that you want right now, then clearly you have not taken the right actions to get the results you want. I know that with the right actions, you can achieve anything and everything you want and this is why this book is going to be so beneficial for you.

You can make a massive difference to your daily habits that will allow you to discover the secrets to earning the money you deserve.

This is what school failed to teach you. If you are willing to put into action the ideas and steps that are laid out for you in this book, I know that you will dramatically improve your current situation. I have had thousands of clients to date who have followed this system, be it through my live events or my online programs, who have transformed their lives. It is my pleasure and privilege to help you get tangible results in your life.

My promise is to deliver step by step systems that will enable you to master the three essential elements, in order to generate more money and success in your life so that you can do what you want to do.

Introduction: Why This Book Will Change Your Life

Now I know you may be sceptical of those words. You may be someone who fears change. You may be someone who is typically hard to convince. You may be someone who believes anything is possible. I appreciate and respect you whatever your model of the world may be.

Notice I use the word 'model' which implies that it is constructed. This means that if you discover how to reconstruct your model to the way you want it, technically you could have, do or be anything you want. Over this short time together, you and I are going to go deep into the most important key driving areas in your life. My intention is always to do my very best for you.

There is nothing more important than being able to attract good things in your life. Knowing you are on the right path means you can see clearly how to get to where you want to be. You can keep those feelings long term so that they get deeper and richer over time.

Behaviourists would argue that our actions are driven either by the concept of wanting to achieve pleasure or avoid pain. We are going to talk about how you can get all the things that you really want in all areas of your life. I would love you to get to a stage where you have bought all the things you've dreamed of buying. When you get to this stage, you'll recognise a higher meaning and purpose for your life beyond those material things. I truly believe that money cannot be the sole answer to anyone's problems.

To be clear, I'm not saying that money is not important. It has its place and needs to be mastered accordingly. I'm sure that you have met someone who has a lot of money and is absolutely miserable. Similarly, I'm sure that you have met someone who has very little money and happy, living life to the full. This clearly defines that happiness cannot be fulfilled by an accumulation of money alone.

Once you have a clear understanding of where you are now and the steps you need to put into place to reach your goal, your level of happiness will elevate rapidly. Maintaining these steps and the momentum will ensure that your future is transformed for good.

At the end of the day, there is nothing more important in your life than feeling good, secure, confident, vibrant and truly happy, on a daily basis, knowing you are clear on your future and have dealt with your past.

Why is the time now to really get this sorted?

Your time is your most valuable asset that you have. Once it's gone, you can never get it back. Being busy myself, I respect your time and I guarantee that by the end of this book, your beliefs around money and time will have dramatically changed. Not only that but they would've changed so much that you'll be able to earn more and spend your precious time more effectively. That is my promise to you.

I have spent my entire working life developing these systems so that they are easy to use and more importantly, so that thousands of my clients, like you, can get the same results that I did. I believe that once you implement what you learn daily, that you'll be blown away by the amount that you can achieve in a very short space of time.

We are living in a unique and exciting time. Never before, has it been so easy to make a massive impact on your life and wealth in a short period of time. There are more and more millionaires created every year, quicker than ever before because of the opportunities in an ever changing environment. It's possible for you to achieve this too, if you're willing to be coachable and take action daily.

If you are just starting out on your journey, I want to reassure you that you are going to get practical strategies and systems to speed up your progress and shave years off your learning curve. Even if you are already pushing your boundaries, are well-read, living the dream and earning to your 'full potential', I'm excited for you too. You know the importance of staying sharp, ahead of the curve and learning daily habits to keep you at the top of your game.

Part 1: Attract

In part one, you will discover how to attract more money and success in your life. It really is simple when you know what to do and there is a process to it. You need a crystal clear step by step system in place to follow. The problem is that a lot of people think they know this and yet they don't have the results that they want. Knowledge is power but taking action gets results.

As Morpheus says to Neo in The Matrix, "There is a massive difference to knowing the path and walking the path." Most people avoid taking action because they are emotionally paralysed by the two formidable emotional challenges in life along the way.

Emotional challenge number 1: Overwhelm

Emotional challenge number 2: Procrastination

Both of these potentially lead to a never ending journey of unhappiness and depression. Unless you master how to destroy these challenges daily, you my friend, are going nowhere fast. I'm a big believer in the law of attraction and maybe you are too? However, I also believe that it can be a little too fuzzy at times. I'm a bigger believer in "The Law of Intention" which states that, "what you put in is what you get out." If you don't have the results you want right now, then quite simply, you haven't put the right actions into place yet.

Whilst on my continued journey of growth through my research for my PhD, I found that it's well documented that the brain needs a clear step by step process when learning. Without it, you just won't get the results or the outcomes you want. You must have a specific, daily intention and a structure in order to attract more money and opportunities in your life. Most people fail in this area because of the lack of structure.

At live events, I'm often asked, "How did you become financially and emotionally free and how do you maintain such a positive balance of happiness at the same time?" My answer is simple, "it comes with mastering the Attract, Acquire and Attain model."

Part 2: Acquire

In part two, you will discover how to acquire more money and success. This really means how to make decisions and choices that are right for you, so that you can find the right path, whilst keeping those challenges overwhelm and procrastination locked away. Now, in this world of mass information, which I believe is only getting worse, making the right choices and decisions is becoming harder for most people.

As overwhelm and procrastination gain momentum, pressure builds up and it becomes harder to move forward. Thankfully this is not how it needs to be. As you go through this book, you'll discover how to make the right decision and save years of your time.

When you know how to avoid making the wrong decisions which cost you a lot more time and money, you'll rapidly become more successful. This will give you the time, freedom and money to do exactly what you want to do.

Warren Buffet said, "If you can avoid making the wrong decisions, you will shave off years from your journey, because when you know the right path for you, the right decisions for you, the right opportunities for you, your journey ahead becomes much clearer, becomes more guided and truly possible."

Part 3: Attain

In part three, possibly the most important part of this book, you'll discover how to attain money and success for the long term.

It's one thing to decide what you want and say that you are going to do it. It takes a completely different skill set to follow through on your actions. Enabling yourself to follow through on your actions is what the third element is all about.

Today, many successful people find it difficult to create and maintain a happy medium between work and life balance. Over the past 10 years I have mastered a work life balance whilst running several profitable businesses and living life on my terms. It is my pleasure to help you on your journey to get exactly that, regardless of where you are now and where you want to be.

I want you to know that whatever you are going through right now and have been through in the past, you are not alone. I look forward to helping you to move forward by changing past references that hold you back. I look forward to you living a happier, fulfilled and free future, living the life that you truly deserve.

How to use this book

I suggest going through this book and doing the tasks daily. Mindfulness is all about being present in the 'now', being aware of your thoughts, feelings and actions. When you read this book, it will be like you and I having a coaching session together daily.

Time is an odd concept and when you have true mastery over it, you will realise it's all just a manmade construct, an illusion. It might be a barrier to doing lots of things in your life. "I just don't have the time, Ed", I hear a lot. However, after completing this book, I know you are going to have the skills to get a lot more time back in your life.

Does it make sense that the only real time we have is the now, our past and our future are perceived concepts of time. It's time to be present with whatever you have in your life now. It's time to take ownership. It's time to become the driver in your life as you will never be as young as you are right now.

You may have friends who blame everyone else for not having the life they want. In ten years' time, when you look back in time to this moment, will you feel proud of what you have achieved or will you wish you were right back here again? Every moment, we have a choice to label each experience as either good or bad, depending on our education, environment, past experiences and our current cognitive training.

So, my friend, let's carpe diem, seize the day. Now is the time to take action and change your future.

TABLE OF CONTENT

PART 1:

PART 2:

ACQUIRE MONEY *93*

PART 3:

ATTAIN LONG TERM WEALTH............................ *153*

CHAPTER 1

ATTRACT MONEY THROUGH MINDFULNESS AND TAKE ACTION DAILY

"Plant the seed of desire in your mind and it forms a nucleus with power to attract to itself everything needed for its fulfilment" - Robert Collie

What is mindfulness?

Mindfulness is defined as the quality of state of being conscious and aware of yourself. It is achieved by focusing on your awareness on the present moment, whilst calmly acknowledging and accepting your feelings, thoughts and behaviours. Many people have the wrong understanding and approach to practicing mindfulness today.

You need focus

Without a focus to guide your thoughts, your thoughts wander all over the place. An inability to keep focused and be aware of what is important, is often the reason for lack of achievement today. Many people don't move forward because they are bombarded with information and feel overloaded, which leads to procrastination and overwhelm. These two emotional challenges are closely linked to depression, which is on the increase.

Take a moment and imagine yourself ten pin bowling. The aim is to roll the ball down the aisle and knock down as many pins as possible in one go. It takes practice, but the challenge in itself is exciting and fun. Not only that, you can measure your progress and success by the frequency and number of pins you knock down. The more time and effort you put into practicing, the more effective and impressive your results are.

Imagine your life is like going ten pin bowling.

Now, imagine going bowling with no pins to knock down? How boring. It wouldn't be fun. There would be nothing to focus on so there would be no point. Imagine that there was no scoring system in place, how would you share the experience with your friends? How would it be enjoyable? There is little point in bowling without something to aim for or something to measure your progress by. Life is no different. If you have nothing to aim for in the beginning and no way of measuring it, what is the point?

You need structure

There is no point to our lives if we're not clear in what direction we're going. Of course, the direction may change as obstacles and challenges appear in our path. Life is like a river, it flows in one direction, it may change course, it may meander in different directions however, it doesn't try to swim back up stream.

Most people fail to direct their lives in a meaningful way because they don't have a clear daily structure in place to follow. Even when they do have some structure, they don't use it on a daily basis because they fail to recognise how helpful it is or don't put it into practice because they think they know better.

My intention is to help you to know and walk your path starting today. I urge you to do the action exercises throughout the book, so that it becomes a visceral experience for you. The more you do, the more hardwired your behaviour and successful daily patterns become. Take decisive daily actions to make a difference in your life rather than just being a passive passenger, waiting for it to drop into your lap.

Many people believe in the Law of Attraction, in fact you may believe in it. Whilst I too believe in the concept, I feel at times it can be a little fuzzy. I'm a bigger believer in the Law of Intention' appreciating that the daily action you take reflects the results you get.

Here's the thing my friend, if YOU don't have the wealth in your life that you truly want,

If you don't have the life of your dreams

If you don't have the level of happiness

If you don't have the body and health

If you don't have the time freedom

If you don't have the money

If you don't have the Job
That you really want

RIGHT NOW...

You need to take action daily

Based on the above, it's clear that until now, you've not put the right daily action into place. I don't want to appear harsh however, for your benefit, it's important that I drive this point home for you. I speak to thousands of people across the world and so many believe that they know everything they need to and yet they don't have the results or life that they really want. Objectively, it's clear to see that they either don't know as much as they think they know or that they have not yet hardwired successful habits and behavioural patterns yet.

You need to be coachable

In the early days when I first started building businesses, I presumed that as I was making more cash than my friends, I knew it all. It wasn't until I failed miserably, found myself with a shed load of debt, having lost a considerable amount of money, that my ego was cut down to size. I am grateful that I learnt that lesson early and became a humble student, learning and adapting constantly on a never ending journey of improvement.

I never claim to know it all. I once listened to the world, famous physicist, Stephen Hawkins and heard him say, "You must remember that when you learn something, to forget it again, so you can re-learn it again and the second time, and the third time and the fourth time it will become stronger inside you."

I remember going back to the bank after I had defaulted on my loan repayments. My plan was to ask them if I could put my repayments on hold and if I could have a little more time to pay back the £500,000 I owed them, because the business had not worked. I was told in no uncertain terms that it didn't work like that. I had to go out and get their money to pay off the debt and take responsibility for my actions.

I learnt more about myself through that single experience than any other experience had ever taught me. It took me 3 years of hard work to pay off the entire debt on my own. I had it hanging over my head every day, like a weight that was dragging me down, however I refused to succumb to its negative energy by staying focused on my end goal.

Implementing the systems in this book, I continued to work my way out of debt and I never looked back. It was a turning point in my life, a defining moment, when I could have given up and turned away from the challenge. I'm sure that you have had moments like this. I'm excited to give you the structures and systems that enabled me to claim back my life and rise like the Phoenix. You too can go and conquer new heights for yourself.

Through our short time together, I'm going to help you engrain these so deep, so you can have more successful results in your life. I'll guide you through clear processes and structures. If you follow step by step, with my help and guidance, you'll not only see rapid results you will also be able to attain them for the long term.

You need direction

If you want to get somewhere today by car, any destination no matter where you are, if you don't know how to get there, then you usually enter the address in your Sat Nav right? No one gets into a car without a clear idea of where they want to go. Let's start by setting your destination and making your intentions clear together. You want to ensure that your Sat Nav system is ready to take you where you want to go and that it's using the most up to date program to avoid unnecessary detours and roadblocks. There's no point in using a system that is old and outdated, which is what most people's personal Sat Nav operates with on a daily basis. Their belief systems are way out of date and in desperate need of an upgrade.

My 'mindful success systems' allow you to attract more money so that you can move forward and more importantly keep you on track as you navigate your path and start living life on your terms. It's vital for you to define what success is for you, as it's very specific for everyone and is an individual goal.

I'm going to share with you my copyrighted Inner DRIVE system ™. It's simple and to the point. I know you might think it's very cheesy however, it's easy to remember and allows a solid foundation to begin our work together. I have used this with my corporate clients, public clients and have also personally used it to design structure over my own thoughts and my mindful actions daily. This has allowed me to consistently move forward and achieve more. Thousands of my clients have rapidly changed their lives by applying the **Inner DRIVE system ™** and once they realise their internal drive, they have more clarity and focus on a daily basis.

Inner DRIVE system ™ will continue to serve you each time you come back to it over and over again. This is something that I strongly recommend you do. Write it out clearly so that you can see it somewhere daily. It was Dr Milton Ericsson, one of the founding fathers of human psychology who stated that all thoughts and memories are started in the brain through a visual trigger. Writing this down so that you can be reminded of it daily is vitally important. I recommend writing it all over your home, your office so wherever you go, you are reminded of your commitments to yourself.

Now I'm not saying this allows everything to fall into place however, it gives us a great starting platform and a system to create forward momentum. It allows you to start understanding how to attract more money and success in your life daily so that you can move forward and get the things you want.

Inner DRIVE system™

D - DECIDE what do you want?

"Ask for what you want and be prepared to get it" - Maya Angelou

Mindfulness is all about being clear and specific about what you want to achieve from your actions on a daily basis. If you are clear about your daily intentions, then in a short period of time, you will see rapid changes in your life. Most people only get motivated and clear once a year on 1st of January when everyone decides that they should set some intentions. Maybe they are at a stage in their life where they have hit a threshold and have had enough of the current pain they're in and want to finally do something about it?

I'm going to help you with some ideas to stimulate your thoughts. Not all of these will be relevant to you right now, however, my aim is to spark a desire inside of you so that you can start to create more of what you want. As you know already, I'm from the UK. People in the UK don't typically say the words "I want" often or easily.

Once you have a clear understanding about what it is that you want, you'll have to grow and develop a sense of worthiness to acquire those wants, in order for that to happen. In UK traditional culture, the concept of "wanting" can be linked to bad things. If you want to help a lot of people, if you want to give away a lot of money, then surely that's not a bad thing?

Many people have very negative beliefs and behaviours around money. My experience and belief is that money is purely a reflection of who you are. People who often have bad associations with money rarely tend to have it in the first place. If you are a bad person and you earn a lot of money, it will only amplify your hidden but present bad qualities. However, if you are a good and generous person, these good qualities will also be amplified.

At an event I was running last year, a member in the audience was talking about Bill Gates, stating that he didn't deserve to have so much money and that it was wrong. I respected his position and his point of view, however, that's not how the economy works. The economy is very simple, if you find a huge problem and solve it, then you'll get paid a lot of money. If you are the first to a market, then you stand a much greater chance of really earning a lot.

Bill Gates is worth as much as he is because he solved a problem that allowed millions of people across the globe to use a computer more effectively and he did it before anyone else. Before Windows was created, the user was expected to know and understand how to code a computer to make it work. Bill Gates made it easier to use and therefore solved a huge problem for millions of people.

Did you know, Bill and Melinda Gates, plan to give away more of their personal fortune than any other country in the world give away today? I cannot see anything wrong with that, can you? Think about some of the major global problems we could resolve today if we all operated at that level? Money won't change who you are, it will only amplify what type of person you are. If you are generous and honest, you'll give more and use your money for the benefit of others. Money is just a vehicle and what you do with it really comes down to you.

Step 1: **DECIDE** what you want and be specific, so that your mind can narrow down on the target. Your power is in making a decision to go after what you want. When you decide that you are going to achieve something, your brain starts to find ways to make that happen.

What do you really want? Do you know? If not, now is the time to think about it and make a decision.

EXAMPLES:

1. I want a healthy, vibrant body and tons of energy
2. I want to be happy and emotionally free of past experiences
3. I want a loving, lasting relationship that makes me feel alive
4. I want more time to do the things I love
5. I want to be an international, motivational speaker
6. I want to earn X amount each month doing what makes me happiest
7. I want to change lives of others by teaching them what I do and know

R - RESULTS recognise what actions you need to take to get the results that you want. This is important, because not only must you uncover what will drive you forward, you must also uncover what it is that you no longer want in your life so that you can avoid it. It's important to remember you are constantly seeking to avoid pain and constantly seeking pleasure in everything you do.

What results do you need to do daily to get what you want? What actions do you not want to do? What results do you not want daily?

EXAMPLES:

I'll invest more time and effort into my skill set

I'll earn more per hour so that I work less or earn more

I'll use my time carefully and get the most out of each day

I'll get up earlier and make time for myself

I won't shy away from learning new skills and hold myself back

I won't say yes to work that doesn't pay what I'm worth and feel undervalued

I won't waste my time on menial tasks and then rush to do what's important

I won't stay up late, go out and then miss my goals

I - IN know what is **IN** the way. It is normal for life to get in the way, so if you are prepared and you can recognise the stumbling blocks you come across often, you can deal with them, and avoid them this time. This is usually a limiting belief or something you have heard said to you many times before.

What obstacles are going to stop you from getting what you want and how can you become more resourceful to deal with this?

EXAMPLES:

Fear of failure

Fear of success

Not earning enough money

Not enough time

Overwhelm

Overweight

I'm not good enough

V - VERY identify what is very important to you right now. As you go through life your priorities change and reflect where you are. Think about what is important to you right now and once fulfilled, your life and success will advance to a whole different level.

To help you, I want to introduce you to a life changing process of even key elements that influence everything you do. Go down this list and find out what your current focus is and where to start.

THE 7 KEY ELEMENTS OF WEALTH ™

Element 1: Health

Element 2: Emotional Management

Element 3: Relationship

Element 4: Time

Element 5: Work/Career

Element 6: Money

Element 7: Legacy

Pick your top 2 so that we can focus on them and we have a clear idea of what is important to you right now. As we spend time going through this book, we will go into much more depth into **THE 7 KEY ELEMENTS OF WEALTH ™** . Mastering them will massively affect your all round fulfilment in life. At the end of the day it's the true barometer for success & fulfilment.

E - EFFECTIVE Decision making. Commit to making the decision that you need to make right now and stick to it. Successful people know that the secret to decision making is to make a decision and then make that decision right. Meaning that once you have made it, you do it no matter what, so that you move forward and make improvements in the area of your focus. Pick one of the elements that you want to improve and make an empowered decision on it.

EXAMPLES:

Get up earlier so I have more time to finish tasks that need to be done.

Eat healthier so I have more energy to get more things done.

Commit to a never ending process of improvement so I can give beyond myself.

Make personal growth a priority so I can have better relationships

Increasing my earning potential daily by investing in my skills.

Push my comfort zone by facing a fear.

Network with some potential opportunities and offer value to them.

Take a moment to think for yourself, take action and write in your own journal.

Fill out **Inner DRIVE system ™** and decide what you want, get clarity and move forward.

D - What do you want?

R - What results do you want & what results do you not want?

I - What's in your way and how can we resolve this now?

V - What's very important to you right now? Pick the 2 most important elements.

E - What's a decision you need to make to move you forward in the direction you want?

Now sometimes people say to me, "Ed I'm not sure what I really want" and that's ok. By going through this journey together you and I are going to get a really clear idea around what is right for you and the path to take. Sometimes people say, "Ed this is stupid, I don't see the point in things like this, how is this really going to help me?"

To that I say "You'll either step forward into growth, or you'll step backward into safety" Abraham Maslow. Abraham Maslow was one of the founding fathers of human motivation. A lot of the work he wrote about was how to advance yourself to reach your human potential, needs, goals and thus become fulfilled and happy. The reason why most people do get lost is because they don't have a barometer to measure their success by. Many successful entrepreneurs talk about the power of guidance and following a structure laid out to achieve more and appreciate where they've come from. Every Entrepreneur, whether it's Richard Branson, Steve Jobs, Bill Gates or Oprah Winfrey talk about the power of having a structure in place and a mentor to help hold them accountable throughout the process. Having a guide to help you stay on track as you follow the steps so that you can move further forward without making the wrong decisions.

Once we discover what the key elements of focus are, then we can start to go deeper into those areas to increase our competency. Most successful people realise that in order to attract more, they must constantly progress and move further forward to avoid hitting the plateau. The plateau is a stage in life where people begin to get stale, bored and the pain body gets activated. In the meantime, those that are successful and continue to reach new heights more often than not, embrace the concept of never ending improvement to attracting more in their life. Now, of course the secret sauce of happiness is not just getting more, otherwise the book would end right here. I'm not sure that the economy really needs a whole lot of people that are just driven by wanting more as well. Of course, it goes a lot deeper than that.

CHAPTER 2

WHY YOUR
PARENTS GOT IT WRONG

HOW TO LEARN FROM
THEIR MISTAKES

Traditionally our parents and grandparents, measured success by the position or job title they held in the economic society. If they went to university, had a professional job, earned a certain amount of money etc, that meant they had a certain level of happiness and success according to the positions they held.

My dad would always tell me, "stick to what you know son, work hard from 9 - 5, come home and watch TV with the family." That is what happiness and success looked like for my dad. Those days were different then. There weren't as many options in those days. You could put money in the bank and get 15 % rate of return on your investment. This would enable people to save money, buy a house and find a level of stability. Those days are most definitely gone! Unfortunately, you cannot get those rates of return from the bank anymore. If you leave money in the bank today, over a 6 year period you will have less money than when you started, due to inflation and the ever increasing living costs that mount up.

Traditional education as a whole, teaches people to become competent in their job. You work your way through the school system, hopefully progressing and then end up working for someone else. If you're lucky, you get some free time in between finishing your working week and the weekend, where you are meant to live your life and have some fun. Then, before you know it, you are retired, hopefully you're still in good health so that you can enjoy whatever time you have left on earth.

Due to the rapidly changing economy, people can't rely on one income stream to provide for their future anymore. There is a huge knock on effect from the economic decisions that have been made such as Brexit and economic problems such as Raising Global Growth, Technology Distribution, Social Cohesion, Geopolitical Threats, Climate Change. These were outlined in a recent article I read in the Telegraph.

Media tends to spread fear and uncertainty around these issues.

People are beginning to realise that more than one income stream is vital because the job market is unreliable, and unemployment is rising. In today's market, if a person or business is not willing to be adaptable and flexible, continue to grow in order to survive, the market with eradicate them.

Darwin's principle rings true now more than ever, "It's not the most successful, it's not the most intelligent, it's not the strongest that survive, but the most adaptable".

When there is fear, people are cautious and worry about the future. Companies are looking at streamlining more effectively and if employees are not adding value to the business, they're looking at ways to either give them more training or find ways to get rid of them and replace them with more valuable employees. As a result, happiness levels in the company go down.

Once businesses have reduced costs, they have started investing a lot of money into employees' happiness and wellbeing. The largest expense to a business is staff turnover.

I have been hired by several different blue chip companies to keep their staff happier and more fulfilled in **THE 7 KEY ELEMENTS OF WEALTH** ™. One of my clients, the Hilton group asked me to run workshops for their directors. The training was on emotional management (Element no 2). Using my unique approach, the directors became more aware of their own emotional intelligence thus allowing them to understand how best to serve their clients and keep them happy! This greatly improved the overall profit and success of the company.

It's well documented that companies like Google, Amazon, Facebook, focus on Element No 4 Time & Element No 6 Money and invest heavily into allowing their staff to choose their time schedules with ROWE (results only working environments). This has been proven to stimulate much happier staff because it puts them in control of their own destiny. It also gets rid of staff that are not willing to put the work in and not be results focused.

It was Virgin who was one of the first companies that looked at ways to empower their staff by allowing as much holiday as they wanted as long as they were willing to hit their targets. What was generally found in most cases was the staff who were more eager, more committed at getting results, wanted to be more successful, were the ones that got more results. Those who took advantage of the rule didn't hit their performance targets and were asked to leave.

Most people today want a better job in some shape or form, be valued more by their employer or dream of having their own business and it becoming hugely successful. Large companies like Facebook and Google noticed this was a key driver and therefore focussed on allowing their employers (once they hit certain targets), to start their own business on the side and allowed an allocation of their paid hours to work on their own business.

Most people in life want to earn more money and/or need more time to spend with their loved ones. I want you to realise this is possible for you too. Today, it's all about the value you provide for your employer. If you're in a job or role in your business and you are not providing a valued service to your clients, then your days are numbered.

Very few people care about Airbnb's and Uber's brand story and how they became so successful. They only care about the service they received from them.

If you want to be more successful, I want you to start thinking about what value you provide at work or in your business. If you're starting a business today, are people really going to get value from what you provide them? Providing great value is the secret ingredient to a winning formula. If you don't add value, then you must be prepared to face hard times. It was Elon Musk founder of Tesla who said, "You get paid in the proportion of value that you offer to the client, solve a big problem and you will make a lot of money."

Look what happened to Blockbuster the DVD/video rental company. They weren't prepared to change with the market and as a result they went BUST. The customer wanted a more efficient way of watching videos. They no longer wanted to pay late fees, they liked the idea of paying a low subscription fee every month to have access to lots of different movies and having instant access. Because Netflix was willing to adapt to the customers' demands, they changed the landscape and an entire new business model was born. The way customers watched videos shifted.

So today, whether you are in a job or you have your own business, if you want to attract more success and get more results in your life, what are you prepared to do to get it? What actions are you doing daily to become more successful? What do you truly give more of, than anyone else at work?

Do you give a better service than your competitors in the market?

Do you provide a better product than your competitors in the market?

Do you deserve your job right now?

Do you deserve a better job?

Do you deserve more money right now?

Do you deserve a more successful business?

Do you deserve to get paid more?

Quick Action Exercise:

Please take a moment for yourself and rate your current actions.

What would you rate yourself?

Deserved   vs   Undeserved

10 9 8 7 6 5 4 3 2 1 0 1 2 3 4 5 6 7 8 9 10

I appreciate what normally happens. Our ego blows up and we overcook it. This also depends on who we compare it to.

It's no good if you compare it to the worst person or the best performer at work.

So, stay humble and give yourself a true score from your heart and then double check it.

Now ask 5 of your closest friends to give you a score. This may feel confronting, but they are objective and love you, so you can trust that their feedback will come from a good place.

This is not judging you, it's giving you a barometer and a gauge, a flag in the ground so that you know you can improve on it over time. I believe a lot of people don't maintain happiness because there's no measuring device, no barometer that they constantly check to see how much they've moved forward. With that in mind, go out and ask 5 people that are not so close to you, to give you a score. The average of your score from those who know you and those who don't will give you a true reflection of your current effort.

So now you have your score, what are you going to do to improve it?

Are there key areas that you could consider to start putting more effort in so that you could get better results out?

What would you consider doing to improve in this area?

List some ideas below:

1. Could you make some choices to eat more healthily, allowing you more energy?

2. Could you go to bed a little earlier, so you could get up earlier?

3. Could you get up a little earlier and be at work first?

4. Could you make use of your time a little better?

5. Could you consider your morning routine?

6. Could you meet up with someone who'll push you out of your comfort zone?

7. Could you rewrite your CV for the job you really want?

8. Could you apply for a new job?

9. Could you offer more value in your role in some shape or form?

CHAPTER 3

THE OLD WAYS OF BUSINESS
ARE LIKE PROSTITUTION

IT'S NOT ALL ABOUT TAKING,
IT'S ALL ABOUT GIVING

It's no longer about beating the competition, business is all about collaboration. The economy is changing and it's vital for us to have a view on this, so you understand the shift and how this will play out for you on your journey, to attracting more happiness and success in your life. Whether you like it or not, you are a part of the global economy and I'm afraid this is something that you will have to get your head around if you want to be successful in today's environment. It's time to realise that the economy is rapidly changing.

At the end of 2017 Toys R Us, one of the largest global toy distributors went bust and there is a vital lesson to be learnt. It would be so easy to label that situation as another victim of the retail industry however, that's not the case. Toys R Us is a result of the rapidly changing way the economy is going and how they became a victim to this. We must continue to remember that, the story behind the brand doesn't really add anything to the brand. Do you ever remember the story of Kodak inventing the digital camera and then doing nothing with it? The situation with Toys R Us is 10 times worse. They had the chance to lead all online toy sales from the very beginning and were on the right track, but they threw it all away.

Just a quick reminder if you don't know the background. Christmas 1999, in the middle of the dotcom boom, when the Toys R Us website was so successful, it was flooded with toy orders and they couldn't ship to all customers on time, leading to a $350,000 fine from the US Federal Trade Commission. They decided to get serious about their online sales. Within two months, by February 2000 they had secured a $60 million investment from SoftBank to grow online. A few months later they announced that they were going to be Amazon's exclusive toy supplier.

Within the first year, the partnership with Amazon led to Toys R Us being the world's top toy site. So far so good. However, soon after they announced their partnership, Jeff Bezos launched Amazon Marketplace, this allowed anyone to sell anything on their site. To the winner-takes-all mentality of companies like Toys R Us, this was a shocking strategy. Other retailers began selling toys not available in Toys R Us, giving customers greater choice. Toys R Us CEO, John Eyler, flew out to meet Jeff for an emergency meeting to force him to stop.

Jeff said, "someone ought to be able to find everything on Amazon - and that by giving more choice to the customer, everyone wins." He pointed to the ongoing increase in Toys R Us sales as a result and said they hadn't broken their exclusivity agreement as none of these new toys were available at Toys R Us.

Jeff added, if they wanted more control, why not give a larger product range? Amazon would then happily make them the exclusive seller on all of the new products they offered as well.

Instead, Toys R Us sued Amazon for breach of contract. John testified, "We are at a point in the relationship with Amazon where we have no trust whatsoever in dealing with this organization." He got a restraining order to try and prevent Amazon selling any other toys on their site. Amazon countersued for "chronic failure" to carry stock of the toys customers wanted. The court case dragged on for five years and eventually Amazon settled with a $51 million payment to get out of the fight.

Toys R Us took their toys and went home, trying to compete with Amazon (and the rest of the Internet) with their own exclusive site, and raising $6.6 billion in a buy out the year after the court case began, in 2005.

Amazon sales went from $2.78 billion when the Toys R Us deal was first struck, to $8.49 billion when Toys R Us sued, to $136 billion last year, making it the fastest company in history ever to reach $100 billion in sales. Toys R Us flatlined on $11 billion in sales in 2016 - the same level of sales they had ten years earlier. Saddled with $5 billion in debt in 2017, Toys R Us filed for bankruptcy.

What set the two companies apart?

It wasn't that one was online and one was offline. It was that one was willing to change, and one wasn't. Jeff Bezos said, "We've had three big ideas at Amazon that we've stuck with and they're the reasons we're successful."

1. Put the customers' needs first

2. Invent

3. Be patient

Imagine if Toys R Us had embraced the same "customer first" philosophy as Amazon?

Imagine if instead of suing, they had listened, experimented and worked together with Amazon? We are living in a world today where the rules have changed. Where it isn't Amazon or Toys R Us that wins. It's the customer that wins. "Throwing the toys out of the pram" isn't the best solution. As Jeff Bezos said, "What we need to do is always lean into the future, when the world changes around you and when it changes against you - what used to be a tail wind is now a head wind - you have to lean into that and figure out what do because complaining isn't a strategy."

Business today has never (until now) become more interlinked with mindfulness behaviour. Business is not about beating the competition anymore. It's all about joint partnerships, finding people that you are aligned with and conquering things together. The one asset you want the most of is time, therefore the quickest way to get more time back is by partnering with people that can speed up your journey.

CHAPTER 4

YOUR SAT NAV IS ONLY AS EFFECTIVE AS THE SOFTWARE

IS IT TIME FOR AN UPGRADE?

Having a clear set of directions is what being mindful is all about. However, we can only operate from our own model of the world based on our experiences. These tend to be guided by our previous background, culture, beliefs and education. Sometimes, people will often ask me, "how do you know you're operating on what's true to you or are you being influenced by your past and by what your parents taught you?" The answer is being truly mindful and becoming aware of the difference between those two thoughts. For example: when you get into a car, you must set the direction for where you want to go. No one ever gets into a car and just drives around without any direction. Those that do, tend to get lost or find themselves without any real purpose or meaning to their journey. You get into a car, put the directions in your Sat Nav (if you're not quite sure where to go), take the quickest route that saves you time or is the most cost effective.

Again, the importance of having someone to guide you is vital, if you want to speed up the process. If you find someone that has been there before, has had the experience, then it's going to speed up the process so that you can get better results in your life too. Find someone who has been on the journey that you desire, who's caring and can nurture your gift, who's happy doing what they're doing and you will go far.

However, if you find someone who doesn't have any results, who is no good at nurturing your gift and isn't happy doing what they're doing, then that's exactly what you'll get too. Choose your mentor carefully to ensure your success.

Think of the directions as a conscious thought. An action that you are in control of. There are many schools of thought about the mind however, most agree that there are 2 key operating components to the mind.

1. Your conscious mind - which is in control of what you focus on, is limited by the fact it can only handle a certain amount

of information/data per second. We call this the goal setter.

2. Your unconscious mind - the much larger section of your mind that is capable of handling a lot more data and is where all your behaviour programs are kept. We call this the goal getter.

It was Freud, one of the first who started looking at these sections of the mind. Although he originally referred to them in different names, he came to the conclusion that it was the unconscious mind that needed the majority of the work.

Conditioning and reconditioning the unconscious mind, enabled people to either get better prepared for the future or realise and change their associations to their past experiences, allowing them to experience a greater sense of purpose and happiness. As time moved on, great thinkers and a variety of schools of thought compounded on these ideas and gave new distinctions to how the mind operated as a whole. This allowed new ways and systems to help people get a better understanding of who they really were and how they could either improve, be happier or more successful in some shape or form.

The positive psychology movement as a whole, was a new way of thinking around studying people. Instead of those who were sick, studying people who had overcome their illness, led to a whole new dimension of thinking, allowing new ways to realize the endless human potential that is now available.

If you study illness, you find out how someone becomes ill rather than how someone becomes better. The key and goal in life is to master these processes by wanting more pleasure and less pain whilst allowing meaning and purpose to continue on a daily basis. By doing this you can attract and acquire more and make the right choices so that you attain long term happiness and success.

It's important to clarify a very important process in the brain. You'll find people that think they know it all. They've read a couple of books, watch a couple of YouTube videos etc and then they think that they have all the information and skills they need to be successful. However, after years of trying, they don't have the results that they want.

The reality is that if people don't have the results that they want, it simply shows that they haven't taken the right action yet. In order to get consistent results, you must take consistent action. Go back to the bowling analogy, the more you consistently practice, the better you become at bowling, the greater your chances are of scoring a strike (all 10 pins knocked down at once).

Bowling is not a game of luck, it's about the number of times you roll the ball down the lane. Success, money and happiness are not things that are ready made. There are things that we have to do over and over again. The more we do it, the easier it becomes because we are conditioned by our experiences and therefore become more effective at doing that behaviour. It becomes a hardwired habit. A habit takes approximately 49 days to become fully automated and each new habit needs to go through 4 key stages before it's hardwired. We need to get you thinking to a level 4 when you no longer need to think about your daily actions because they've become hard wired.

The 4 key stages of behavioural development

So You Can Attract Consistent Results in Your Life

Increasing your money and achieving success is the result of our behaviours, actions over a period of time, supported by a positive, empowering environment.

Four key stages to learning a new skill

First stage: Unconscious Incompetence

This is where you don't know what you don't know and it's a very dangerous place to be. If you start a business at this stage, then be prepared to lose a lot of money. This is the stage when you get introduced to the car for the first time. You have no understanding of how to operate it. When you sit in the car, you're completely unaware of how to use the different controls simultaneously so that you can move forward.

Quick Action Exercise:

If you want to be a racing car driver and learn to drive more effectively, you get a world class teacher/mentor to help you. You pay your teacher/mentor for their services and commit to a level of training. You opt for either:

Bit by bit learning – where you take one lesson a week. This is the slowest form of training, perhaps you learn this new skill with your dad?

Immersion learning – this is the process where you immerse yourself in a learning process for a set period of time with a trained professional. This is the fastest, most effective way to acquire the new skill, get it hardwired into your brain so it becomes conditioned as a faster behaviour.

Quick Riddle:

Student A: opts for bit by bit learning process with their father, who is untrained.

Student B: opts for immersion learning process with a professional, experienced teacher.

Who learns the skills faster?

Student A or

Student B

Bit by bit learning means, having one driving lesson a week for a year until the student passes. Immersion learning means, having an intense learning experience for 4 days to allow the student to pass.

Who is the better driver at the end of a year?

Student A:

Student B:

Student B would most likely be a better driver because they passed their test sooner, allowing them to gain more experience over the course of the year. Student A would spent the whole year learning to drive and only then would they gain more experience.

Based on this process I recommend going through this book as quickly as possible and blocking out your time to do it. Ideally, if you could go through it several times and apply the action steps simultaneously, you would get a lot more from the process than just reading a little bit at a time. I have ensured it's a simple, straight forward, jargon free book so that you can go through the material faster, apply it daily and start seeing results straight away. If at a later stage (only if it's right for you), you're serious about investing in yourself, you might be interested in purchasing some of my online training courses which are designed to help you achieve more in less time.

Second Stage: Conscious Incompetence

You become aware of what you don't know. This is the stage when you sit in the car and you're taught how to operate the car and you suddenly realise how little you really know. At this stage, you might get upset and overwhelmed due to the amount of information brought to your awareness.

Quick Action Exercise:

You apply more learning at this stage to advance to the next stage.

Learning is still not free flowing and can take up a lot of head space to process the new concept.

People sometimes give up at this stage because they think they know it and find it easier to stop than to continue because of the potential pain in undertaking a new skill.

Third Stage: Conscious Competence

You become good at the specific behaviour however, it still takes up a lot of your processing data and you have to consciously think about what you're doing. This is the stage before your driving test. You're aware of the right actions to take to get the car moving forward however it drains a lot of energy.

Quick Action Exercise:

At this stage, a lot of people give up because they think they know it however as they continue to move forward, this is where true mastery occurs.

Fourth Stage: Unconscious Competence

This is where you become habitually conditioned with the new behaviours and it becomes automatic. You have become it and you are it. This is the stage where you are driving the car, talking to your friend, not thinking about what your feet are doing all at the same time. The behaviours are automatic and deep in your unconscious mind.

In essence if we take these simple daily actions, my core belief is that anyone can get anything they want in life, if they're willing to commit to a period of time where they train any thought and action into stage 4 so that it becomes hard wired.

Every action and behaviour must go through these 4 stages to become a habit. This principle is key. As one takes one action and behaviour, they keep compounding on top of it until it becomes hard wired and programmed at level 4 Unconscious Competence. It takes around 49 days to get a new habit to stick permanently and that depends on how many times they have attempted it before and the intensity they commit to ingraining the new behaviour.

People often ask me, "Ed I know this, I have read loads, how come this isn't automated yet?" The answer is simple. "You have to continue improving your skills so that it becomes an automatic behaviour, you need to keep practising the action or behaviour. Get a strong environment to condition your behaviour and do some cognitive retraining. This cannot be done on your own."

When learning something new, it's not enough to just know it. It must be automatic. Most people give up at either stage 2 or 3. At stage 3 when someone has a critical moment in their life, they either give up or dig down deep and the action/behaviour goes to stage 4.

People often ask me, "how long does it take to get a skill from stage 1 to stage 4?" It depends on the age of the person, how much they've done before, whether the action or behaviour is new and lastly how determined and willing the person is.

CHAPTER 5

TO ATTRACT MORE YOU MUST BECOME MORE

FROM THE INSIDE OUT

I appreciate that today most people think talking to ourselves is a crazy concept. However, if you watch someone walking down the road more often than not, you'll see them talking to themselves. We all have an inner logical voice that questions our action and this isn't necessarily a bad thing at all. The logical element in our brain must be convinced in order to make a decision and move forward. However, the problem is that most people's logical inner voice, is and can be, their worst critic.

Training your inner voice

We all have an inner voice. If you don't believe me, you may have said to yourself "there is no voice in my head" and unintentionally proved my exact point. It's that little voice that I'm referring to. Would it be fair to say that by managing your inner voice, you would be able to align your thoughts and feelings with intended behavioural patterns and actions? You must exercise and practice this daily to see rapid results and changes in your life.

It was Aristotle who said, "We are what we repeatedly say and do." What do you repeatedly tell yourself? People who don't believe this concept will say that it's all BS, however they will often happily tell themselves disempowering statements like "I'm not good enough", "I always fail", "I can't be happy", and yet they are surprised when they get those exact results.

I'm sure you've met someone who continually says to themselves "I'm tired" and low and behold they find themselves feeling tired every day. If they were just to change the statement to a positive command such as "I need more energy" and the unconscious mind would go about presenting ways to make that a reality.

Daily practice will condition and create a better emotional state thus you will be more able to deal with the challenges you face more effectively and become more successful. This doesn't mean that all your problems will go away instantly but, you'll be able to attract more success by creating successful habits. The most significant of which is your morning mindfulness mantra.

Attract More Success Daily With a Morning Mindfulness Mantra

M - Morning - Think about how productive your entire day will be if you start it feeling focused, positive and empowered as soon as you wake up. This is the purpose of a mantra and the reason why it's most effective when you do it as soon as you wake up. The more you practice this, the quicker you'll get used to it and this in turn will build a new program for your brain to automatically follow. Even if you've had very little sleep, but then again probably more so, doing this morning ritual will set you up to hit the ground running. Make a point of creating space and time to support and cultivate a strong mindset for the best possible emotional state every day and you'll be shocked at how much more you get out of the day.

A - Assertive command - Your morning mantra is your war cry, it's what lights the fire in your belly to get up, get out and get your stuff sorted. It should inspire and energise you, so it needs to be powerful which is why it's an assertive command.

If you tell yourself a command daily that empowers you, you'll feel more confident and ready to do what it takes to reach your goals. Think about the people in your life who are go getters, 'naturally' successful and consider how often they tell themselves disempowering mistruths - they don't, do they?

As you become more aware of your internal commands, you'll be able to change them so that they serve you, rather than hold you back. Test what works for you by trying out different assertive and powerful statements. Start with what feels right and as you begin to feel more comfortable and confident you can adjust it. For example, for years I've been telling myself daily, "Every day and in every way, I'm getting stronger and stronger and stronger." You can start with this and notice how you feel versus how you feel if you were to say the opposite, "Everyday in every way, I'm getting weaker and weaker and weaker" and notice what happens. You can also simply test how different you feel when you repeatedly tell yourself "I can do this" versus "I can't do this" especially if you're out for a run or doing something challenging.

It's different for everyone but most people notice that when they say I can and repeat it over and over the following is likely to happen:

You notice that your shoulders go back

You notice that you hold your head higher

You notice that your breathing gets deeper

You feel more centred

You feel stronger

You feel a sense of power

You feel empowered

Now I'm not saying that this alone will enable you to run a marathon without ever training or be able to run up a mountain without any prior practice. What you'll notice is well documented by many successful sports athletes, they know what they say will be experienced in the body and so I want you to start realising that the mind and body is intermittently connected as one and what you say and think is felt throughout your body. Sometimes, for a non believer approach, its best if you wait until you're tired from a run and then at a peak moment when you could either stop or keep going, test how what you say to yourself, influences how you feel and the results you get.

For many years, the effect of what you say and think on your physical body was merely suspected. It was proven by Otto Loewi when they found that neurotransmitters throughout the entire body allow electrical messages to be passed from the brain to every cell in the body. Before this discovery, it was thought that the brain was separate from the body. They couldn't figure out how the electrical charge from the brain passed over the synaptic gap and into the body. Today, the mind body connection is well recognised and not just a hokey pokey concept that alternative medicine therapists recognise and contemplate.

Quick Case Study:

One of my first studies in psychology when I was doing Sports Science for one of my A levels was this experiment.

As the student is about to give up they either say "I can" or "I can't".

Every time I tested it, with a range of students and similar conditions each time

the results were the same.

The students that said "I can" ran for longer.

The students that said "I can't" gave up sooner.

Then I swapped the groups over and time and time again the students got the same results.

Each time at the peak of threshold. Those who had the positive command of "I can" ran for a longer period of time and beat themselves and their previous experiences when they used "I can't."

Choose a positive command to say to yourself on a daily basis, at the start of the day and throughout the day, whenever you want or need a burst of confidence, energy or focus.

Here's a list of some of my positive commands and personal mantras:

God's wealth flows in my life in an avalanche of abundance

I am powerful beyond all measure

I am confident, calm, cool and collected

I am real, raw and ready

Everything I need is within me now

I can handle it, I can handle it, I can always handle it

I am a champion

The list goes on and on.

I personally prefer quick and short commands. I focus on some core statements and one big mantra daily, that has a rhythm to it and I say it over and over again to myself.

Quick Action Exercise:

I think it's more important for you to develop what is right for you.

Take a moment and think about what would be right for you?

I am ......

Now your test is to see if you can say it daily until it becomes hard wired in you until it becomes 'Unconsciously Competent' inside of you like we discussed in the previous chapter.

The more you do it, the better you'll get at it and the easier your life will become.

Feel free to use one of mine, and if I were to suggest one it would be

Every day, in every way, I am getting stronger and stronger and stronger.

N - New Belief - The point of a mantra is to help you install a new belief and a new way of thinking. I'm not saying just by simply telling yourself that you'll automatically believe something completely different about yourself. However, every child believes in the tooth fairy because they were told by a parent that the tooth fairy was real. They chose to believe it and at a later stage in life they realised that it wasn't real anymore.

If you tell a child they are slow, stupid and unloved then they'll believe it and never realise that it was untrue as well. My point is that what you tell yourself repeatedly over time, is what you will begin to believe about yourself.

Tell yourself good things and you'll begin to believe in good things in time. However, this needs to be supported by the right environment, the right people who will support and help you become the best version of yourself. Be mindful of who you spend your time with. If you spend time with those who don't embrace your views of wanting to be the best version of yourself by replacing old, limiting beliefs with new beliefs, the new seed of thinking won't even get a chance to embed a single tiny root before it's killed.

Quick Action Exercise:

Consider the people in your life who are supportive and encouraging. Look to spend more time with them as you develop a new set of empowering beliefs about yourself and abilities. Who can you spend more time with daily that will empower you more?

T - Tempo and Rhythm - There must be a tempo and rhythm to your mantra to help it stick in your mind. Most people remember the nursery rhymes they grew up with, however, when they attempt to remember something in today's world they struggle because there's no structure to the new concept or belief. If you put a rhythm to your mantra, it will engrain deeper into your unconscious mind and stick much stronger.

Again, test it out and see if you find it works for you. There's a lot of research around tempo and rhythm and for centuries different religions have used songs, rhythm, to create a new way of thinking. Take this concept and apply it to yours.

When I say mine,

"Every day in every way I'm getting stronger and stronger and stronger." I focus on accentuating the different words in the sentence so that it feels different inside of me every time I say it.

Quick Action Exercise:

Focus on saying the statement below over and over again. Each time change the emphasis on the word and notice what happens, notice what you feel inside, notice how the tension inside you changes.

For example: first focus on the,

EVERY DAY in every way I'm getting stronger and stronger and stronger!

Then focus on the,

Every day IN every way I'm getting stronger and stronger and stronger!

Then focus on the,

Every day in EVERY WAY I'm getting stronger and stronger and stronger!

Then focus on the,

Every day in every way I'M getting stronger and stronger and stronger!

Then focus on the

Every day in every way I'm GETTING stronger and stronger and stronger!

Then focus on the

Every day in every way I'm getting STRONGER and stronger and stronger!

Then focus on the

Every day in every way I'm getting stronger and STRONGER and stronger!

Every day in every way I'm getting stronger and stronger and STRONGER!

Test this out as part of your morning routine and let me know how you get on with it.

I'm not saying that it will solve all your problems, however it will begin to start a new cycle of behaviours inside you, creating positive momentum and the ripple effect, the domino effect into all areas of your life. Over a period of time you'll either become more empowered and positive based on a couple of primary actions or you'll become more disempowered and negative over a couple of primary behaviours. The choice is yours.

R - Repetition - The repetition helps your mantra become hard wired into the deeper part of your brain. We learn new skills quickly and effectively by constantly repeating it over and over again and the brain knows this very well. Most of our bad behaviour is created by thoughts and feelings that we repeat over and over again to ourselves. As you repeat positive commands, they'll become more present in your daily actions and behaviour. Most people buy into this as a concept yet don't do it enough to get consistent positive results.

A - Always - When should you do it? Always. Many people say, 'Ed, I tried it for a bit. I also tried it just before doing a presentation at work and I didn't get the result that I wanted.' So, here's the thing, you need to do it daily in order to be able to dip into it just before you encounter a pressured experience. When you practice your mantra daily, it works in every situation. If you don't practice your mantra daily, you can't rely on it when it really counts. You're creating a new behaviour, a new powerful command that your body will respond to. I practice my mantra daily to harness the most positive and effective emotional state. It also keeps me sharp and strong so that I can handle any challenge the day brings.

Quick Action Exercise:

Commit to a period of time at least 49 days. Which is 4 weeks. Getting up 10 minutes earlier, walking outside wherever you are in the world. 49 days is about the optimal time to start changing a habit and for a new wiring to becoming a more automated program in the brain.

Step 1: Warm up your breathing with 4 sharp breaths going in and 4 sharp breaths going out.

This will get your energy up and your temperature up. It'll also start pumping oxygen around your body more effectively.

Step 2: Whilst putting your hand on your heart, rub your heart and think about all the things that you can be grateful for. Focusing on an image of gratification is very important at the beginning of the day to flood your senses with bursting amounts of grateful thoughts that you already have in your life. Do this for at least 3 minutes whilst your breathing is slow, steady and deep.

Step 3: Whilst still rubbing your heart, focus now on love and sending it out into the world and to you to heal the situations, the people that need it the most. Give it from a space of just pure love where you're not worried about getting anything in return. Do this for at least 3 minutes again.

Step 4: Whilst rubbing your heart, focus now on 3 key actions that you can do today to get yourself further forward. What are the key 3 actions that you can to get yourself further forward?

Note what they are and start increasing your breathing again. Back to the 4 breaths in and 4 breaths out. If you need to pace up and down, you can or stay still whatever is best for you.

Step 5: Last step one minute over and over again saying with assertive energy your statement and command and practice really saying it like you mean it. Practice saying it with conviction. Practice really believing it and notice how you feel in that moment.

I want you to give this a go.

I totally respect wherever you are in life, whatever you think. In order to get a different result from the results you are currently getting, you have to be willing to try something different and approach it from a different angle. The key is to put yourself in the most positive empowering and emotional state each day, so you can handle the daily challenges that arise.

Test it out and score below how good you feel right after it.

Note that if you put very little effort into your morning mantra, you simply can't expect to get a lot of motivation out of it.

Rating

1-10 How good did you feel straight after your morning mantra experiment?

CHAPTER 6

MASTER THE LAW
OF ATTRACTION

MASTER YOUR
UNCONSCIOUS MIND

Your unconscious mind is fascinating. As you delve deep into your unconscious, you will discover how to get rid of your negative emotions that you experienced in the past thus allowing you to create more in your future and become more successful and live a life of wealth and happiness.

The more you put into this area, the more successful you will become. The mind is the key to your full potential. I like to think of your unconscious mind as a **DRAGON ™**. The more you train your **DRAGON ™** the more success and results you'll attract in your life. The dragon is a wonderful concept. With the right trainer you can get your dragon under control and this has great power. With no training or the wrong training, your dragon can turn against you and eat you alive.

Take for example the movie Avatar. Jake Sully, the underdog has let the whole of the Navi tribe down. In order to prove his worth to his new family, he captures the greatest, deadliest and wildest dragon "Toruk Makto" and becomes a hero. One of the best scenes in the movie is when Jake Sully flies down amongst his new people riding "Toruk Makto." This symbolises that he has been awakened and is the chosen one!

The more you train your mind, the more you'll realise its full potential. Your mindset will either support you in getting the things you want, or it will work against you. The choice is yours.

Programming your DRAGON ™ with

D DIRECT: Positive commands. Tell your unconscious mind exactly what you want it to do. I want to get up early. I am powerful beyond all measure. I want to earn a certain amount of money per year.

R REPETITION: Your unconscious mind responds with commands that are repeated over and over again. You must keep repeating commands until they stick in your mind. The more you do it, the easier it becomes. Most people fail or give up too easily training their mind effectively.

A ASSERTIVE: Each command must be said in an assertive and direct positive command. The more energy you put into the command, the more you will get out of it.

G GOVERNS: Your unconscious mind governs 90 % of your behaviour, holds your positive and negative emotions. It manages and controls the majority of your bodily functions. Think of your conscious mind as being the rider on the dragon, in control of the super powerful dragon beneath.

O ONLY: Least resistance. Your unconscious mind wants an easy way out or the quickest route to a solution. It is always looking for an easy option to get out of doing something difficult. You must understand this when you want to train your unconscious mind effectively. The more effectively you train your unconscious mind, the stronger it will become.

N NEGATIVE: Negative commands kill your dragon over a period of time. They slowly eat away at your dragon's skill, confidence and general ability to perform any task. This will eventually lead your dragon getting stuck deep in the CAVE ™ a concept which we will explore a bit later in the book.

The law of attraction and focusing on positive thoughts

If you train your **DRAGON ™**, you will stand a much greater chance of attracting the things that you want in life. However, there is a difference to thinking about something and taking action. Your **DRAGON ™** needs strong action commands to respond in the best way possible.

I think of the law of attraction like this. You must hold a positive representation of the things that you want to achieve. You can use **The DRIVE ™ System** get more clarity and focus. If you were a magnet, you would hold magnetism inside of you. If a piece of metal is on the other side of the room, outside your magnetic field, it doesn't matter how positive you are, the metal isn't coming to you unless you begin to move toward it and do your part, bringing it closer into your magnetic field so you can start attracting it to you. The more you practice daily, the better you'll become.

When I was younger, I tested this theory out. I wanted to buy a new Porsche (boys and their toys!) I wanted to impress the girls. I grew up in a poor area and this represented success and a great sense of achievement for me. I put buying a new Porsche in The Inner DRIVE system and I decided that was what I wanted to buy. I circled a date in the diary and decided when it was going to happen by. I put daily action steps into place to produce the results I wanted and did them consistently. I was 22 when I set that intention and every day I worked hard to make it a reality. I set a date for it to happen and I achieved it 5 years earlier than expected.

I could've given up on so many occasions. I set my intention and broke down the steps of exactly what action I needed to take. The steps were very specific. One of which was to increase my hourly rate and as a by-product, buy a new Porche. Even though I had set myself a goal of buying my Porche in 8 years, it surprisingly only took me 3 years to achieve! I had also decided that an asset would pay for my car as I didn't want to pay for it from my active income. This step is vital and something successful entrepreneurs do all the time. I created assets that paid for my liabilities and continue to do so today.

It doesn't mean to say that because you purchased a new car everything in your life will be better. However, it's great to have a starting point, whatever feels right for you. The more money you attract into your life, the more you are able to pay your overheads, become more financially secure and help more people along the way. You can start giving on a much larger scale and really making a difference in the world.

So, I tell you this because I believe in your unlimited potential. I believe in you more than you probably believe in yourself. I tell you this not to brag or impress you, I tell you this to inspire you to do great things. It really is possible when you apply what is in this book.

Quick Action Exercise:

Practice training your dragon

1. Fill in the blank and finish the sentence with something inspiring 'I am …!' 'I am strong!''

2. When practicing your mantra you must repeat it over and over again.

3. Practice your Relax and Release, followed by some assertive powerful statements that you tell yourself.

4. Focus on the hardest tasks first. This should be done in the morning. This is when your brain has the most energy. As you do more difficult tasks, you'll become a champion and realise that no tasks are too hard.

5. Become aware of the negative commands that you tell yourself and eradicate them from your vocabulary.

CHAPTER 7

TO ATTRACT MORE YOU
MUST BELIEVE MORE

DEFINE WHAT SUCCESS
MEANS TO YOU

Our belief systems come from our culture, background, education and past experiences. Most people need an upgrade in their personal development to fit into today's society.

Your belief structure is like the software in your sat nav. If you haven't upgraded in a while, it will slow you down or take you off the beaten track, rather than the most direct route. I respect that your current beliefs, your background, religion and what your parents have taught you to date greatly influence your outlook and decision making. The only thing I ask is whether your beliefs consistently empower or disempower you? If your answer is the latter, I would encourage you to consider a new way of thinking if you want to be more empowering to yourself and others.

Have you considered your beliefs around money and success? Perhaps this is something new to you and you've not considered it before? Would it be fair to say that traditional education doesn't offer wealth building classes?

Many people in the UK have very poor beliefs around money. I know many parents who have told their children, "Money is a bad thing, money doesn't grow on trees, money is the root of all evil" etc, etc. What you do with it is all that counts. Money is synonymous with freedom to choose how you live your life and the impact it has on those around you. Choose to use it for good and you'll change your beliefs around earning money.

I would love to help you get a positive experience around money by taking you through The 7 Key Beliefs you need to master financial freedom. **The SUCCESS ™ belief system**. Thousands of my clients have changed their association with money by going through this system and because of it, have rapidly increased their earnings and given a lot more away to great causes. Money is very important in the world. Without it, we can't live or survive today. Having a healthy relationship with money is vital if you want to live the life you truly deserve.

Financial Freedom SUCCESS Belief system ™

S - **SERVE** people what they want daily, you will earn a lot more.

U - **(U) YOU** are in control of your mind and only you will make yourself rich.

C - **COMMUNICATION** is the response you get. What you give is what you get.

C - **CASH** (money) does grow on trees.

E - Money is **EVERYWHERE** and everyone has all they need to achieve any goal inside them.

S - The **SIGNAL** under all negative emotion is the key to all change.

S - The **SECRET** to earning money is to know it can always be made and there is no such thing as failure.

Let's break it down into more detail so that you can take action and start to see results more clearly and quickly.

S: SERVE Others Daily What They Want & You Will Earn A Lot More

If you find out what people want and need and give it to them, you'll have the winning business formula. All successful businesses commit to outstanding service. Business is all about finding the problem and providing a solution. If you want to make a lot of money, find out what people need, offer a low price solution and you'll hit the jackpot.

When I started working for myself, I worked for free. I loved helping people. It was only when my dad said that I had to make this a viable business, that I began to charge for my time. If I couldn't pay rent what was the point of helping others? I went through the process of learning to appreciate the value I offered to my clients. The more value I offered, the greater value I perceived in myself. The journey was slow, however as I improved, I got better results and got paid more and more. The more people I helped, the better I felt about myself. New opportunities opened up and I started doing joint ventures and creating other businesses with my clients.

It has been proven many times that seeking individual pleasures vs helping others, is far greater when you focus on helping others. Michael Steger, a psychologist at the University of Louisville in Kentucky did a test group where he measured pleasure seeking behaviours vs meaningful activities helping others. He measured these daily tasks over a 3 week period.

In the first experiment he found that the more the test candidates participated in meaningful activities, the happier they were. They felt their lives had more purpose and therefore were more motivated and productive than pursuing their own goals. However, this experiment had flaws in the research. They didn't take into account that some people might have felt guilty about reporting pleasure seeking behaviours. So, with this insight, Steger modified the research process.

They prepared a new group of students to perform the study again, this time over a longer period of time. The psychologist got the same results. They did it again. They got the same results again. They did it several times over, each time with a new test group and again they got the same results. The more the people involved participated in meaningful activities, the happier and more purposeful their lives felt and as a result, they achieved more towards their personal goals.

Quick Action Exercise:

Today what action can you take to go out of your way to help someone else?

Can you consistently help someone else on a daily basis? Give yourself a score 1 -10, how would you rate your daily actions in service and caring for others?

U: (U) You are in control of your mind and only you will make yourself rich

You are in control of your mind and thus your results. No one else will ever make you rich. If you're waiting for someone else to come along and solve your problems, then you'll be waiting a long time. If you're waiting to win the lottery so that you can pay off your debts, then you'll be waiting a long time. There is a lot of evidence about people who won the lottery and ended up losing it all, becoming depressed and resorting back to their old unhealthy habits. The reason is that because they didn't earn the wealth, they didn't have the skills to keep it or manage it properly. Many of those studied lacked purpose and drive because financial success was handed to them on a plate and there was no self worth or pride attached to their financial freedom.

You are in charge of your mind. There are a lot of people who are completely unconscious and unaware of their behaviours. The more aware you are of your brain's ability to control your reality, the more aware you become of the things you say to yourself on a daily basis. You can begin to create your own reality and stop your past from holding you back. It is well documented that people who get up early every morning achieve more during the day, tend to be higher earners.

Quick Action Exercise:

What command do you tell yourself just before you get up in the morning?

What is it?

Notice the command and write it down.

If you are an early riser, I bet your morning command is a lot more empowering than someone who presses the snooze button every morning.

Most people have a command of, "oh no not another day" or "just one more minute" then that minute leads to another and then another. What happens is you end up training your brain to not get up. You are in charge of your brain and thus your results.

Quick Action Exercise:

I want you to practice a new command in the morning to get up a little bit earlier. As your alarm goes off, I want you to notice your eyes open. Your body will begin to test itself and check your body to see if it's working. At that moment, do a count down like a rocket ship. I know, I know, it's cheesy to do this. It has been proven that the body and mind react very strongly to number countdowns. Give it a go, you have nothing to lose. Start with a 5 second countdown to 1.

At 5 - open your eyes

at 4 - push the duvet down

at 3 - tense your whole body

at 2 - swing your feet onto the floor

at 1 - shout let's go!

I guarantee you'll start the day quicker and your partner (if you have one) is guaranteed to think you are completely crazy. Everybody has an internal command just before they get up. Most have "I'm tired" not realising that their own command is what's making them even more tired.

C: COMMUNICATION is a sign or response you get back.

What you give is what you get back. What you put out will come back to you in some shape or form. I know some peop e won't believe it, so test the principle. When you're in the car, stuck at the traffic lights, turn and look out the window at the car next to you and raise your middle finger. Notice their reaction. People will probably be shocked, get really angry and possibly give you the middle finger back. Then give them a smile with your hands shaped like a heart. The person you are signalling to, will most likely laugh or smile back at you with a heart shaped gesture too – here's hoping anyway.

Once we take ownership over this belief then we can truly start to take our life and success to a whole different level. Imagine that you're in the centre of your universe and everything starts and finishes with you, including all positive and negative behaviours.

If you're angry in your daily activities, then you'll get back anger based responses. Practice giving away your money. When I was very young one of my first mentors advised me to give 10 % of my money away. I thought to myself, how am I ever going to do that I have so little already? He said, "if you can't give away 10 % of £10, how are you going to give £100 from £1000, £100,000 from £1 million?" You get used to giving your money so that you don't have a scarcity mindset. If you give 10 % of your money away, this sends a message to your brain that there's plenty for everyone and allows you to back up the momentum and make more money.

Distributing your money every month is essential. I've noticed my clients who've done this have grown their accounts substantially. This is how you should split your salary up each month.

10 % of your monthly salary give away to a charity or a good cause. You will feel good because you will be doing good. Come from an abundant mindset rather than a scarcity mindset.

20 % of your monthly salary re-invest into your skills and your personal growth. Your skill set is the most important asset you have. The more you increase your skills, the more you'll earn.

20 % of your monthly salary use to pay your overheads. Your rent, your food, your phone bill. Get rid of your TV and focus on education through means which you control. Podcasts, books, audios and courses. Keep your living costs as low as possible. Most entrepreneurs learn to live very simply whilst they're building their businesses.

20 % of your monthly salary save to invest into growth schemes. This might be higher risk so be prepared to potentially lose this amount. However, the reward may be worth the risk. Make sure you calculate your risk vs your return.

20 % of your monthly income hold for fun times and the dream purchases.

10 % of your monthly income put into a super safe security bond that will always be there for you. Just in case.

Quick Action Exercise:

1. Practice giving out different energy for the day. Spend a whole day in a low energy mood and stay in that mood. Put on a sad face. Talk slowly and in dull tones and notice what sort of responses you get back in return.

2. Practice giving out a higher energy, a more positive upbeat vibe. Talk with more passion, integrity and lust for life and notice what you get back in return.

3. Practice giving a better level of service, give more of yourself at work, outperform your competitors in the market and go beyond what people expect of you and see what you get back in return.

C - CASH money does grow on trees

Money does grow on trees but only if you plant the right seeds. My dad used to tell me that money doesn't grow on trees. I disagree and believe that if you plant the right seeds, then money really does grow on trees. If you're willing to invest in yourself and upgrade your skills, then you'll reap a greater harvest.

Your mind is your greatest asset. If you want a healthy, lean and sexy body then you go to the gym. Once you've achieved what you want, if you stop, you'll go back to what you were before. Maintenance is key. Your brain is a muscle that must be trained on a daily basis. The more you train it, the better it becomes, the faster it will operate for you. When you grow any tree, plant high quality seeds, make sure you water and look after it daily to create the best possible fruit and then my friend, you'll grow a beautiful money tree.

Quick Action Exercise:

How often do you take in new content?

How often do you listen to podcasts?

How often do you attend live events?

How often rather than just talking about your idea, do you invest in your idea and move it forward?

E - Money is EVERYWHERE when you realise that all business is just a solution to a problem

You get paid in proportion to the number of problems you solve in the market. The deeper the problem, the more pain someone is in, the more they're willing to invest to get the problem resolved.

For example: you suspect there is a leak in your tap. You are not really motivated to call a plumber so you leave it. The tap begins to drip more. You notice a pool of water on the floor and you suddenly think I must call a plumber. You clean the floor, the tap stops dripping, you get distracted and you forget about it. Some people might get a plumber around at this point to have a look at the tap. The desire to call the plumber has diminished. Suddenly the tap bursts, water goes everywhere. There is now a strong desire to get a plumber in as quickly as possible to fix the problem immediately. Bill Gates founded Windows, which enabled the world to access a computer and use it. Before he created Windows, if you wanted to use a computer, you would have to understand coding. He was first to the market, found a problem and gave the world his solution.

Quick Action Exercise:

Even if you are in a job right now, what problems do you resolve at work?

How could you become better at doing this?

If you want to start something on the side, what problem do you want to resolve?

S: The SIGNAL under the negative emotion is the key to all change

Imagine if underneath every negative emotion there was a signal or warning. Instead of pretending and living in denial that the emotion wasn't there or trying to avoid experiencing that emotion. If we took a moment and learnt from that action signal, we would discover what that emotion was telling us. This would allow us to take control of our emotions and be happier and more successful in the future.

It was Freud who wrote in 1929 "Civilisation and Its Discontents". Most people find life too hard to deal with and don't know how to deal with negative emotions. A lot of Behavioural Psychologists believe that we are purely driven by pain and pleasure.

Most people will do either 1 of 4 things when a negative emotion is felt in the body.

1. Deny the negative emotion

They will either deny the experience completely or pretend it never happened. The negative emotion gets locked away in the unconscious mind and builds up over a period of time. If a person keeps on denying their emotions, they'll end up coming out at a later stage in life when they least expect it. The common phrase "having a mid-life crisis" is merely a build-up of negative emotions that have been denied for an extended period of time and have been triggered by a pain in life where that person finally cannot handle any more of that particular stimuli.

2. Avoid the negative emotion completely or avoid the situation where the negative emotion is felt

Most people when they've had a bad breakup will avoid putting themselves into that situation again because they link huge pain to the process of relating to another person. Some will avoid this for the rest of their lives. Take public speaking, most people develop an early fear about standing up in public. They often link a negative emotion to it initially and it ruins their growth. This is because they're not taught how to manage this experience correctly. For years I've taught thousands of people to get over their fear and convey their message with confidence and charisma.

3. Compare the negative emotion

Comparing is an interesting process in the brain. The negative emotion gets us "off the hook" and therefore avoid the message underneath the experience. "You look like you have gained a little weight" "You should see my friend, they are much worse than I am" "I used to be a lot worse than I am now". Comparison statements don't allow us to take the message on from the perceived negative emotion. As a result, we avoid the pain and find comfort in knowing it's not too bad.

4. Learn from the action signal

Underneath every negative emotion or signal there is a message to learn. If we find out the warning or signal, we can become much stronger because of it. Most people don't want to feel fear. They'll do their best to deny the emotion and pretend it's not there. They avoid any circumstance where they feel it, and if faced with the emotion, they do their best to compare their experience, so they can feel better about themselves. However, if we discover the message underneath the emotion, we become more prepared and end up in the driving seat.

Your ability to move forward will be blocked by fear. People who are successful don't like the term fear so they re-label it as stress, when in actual fact they are one and the same. If you want to earn more, fear will be the one block in your way that will stop you from asking for a raise, stand up to your boss or start your own business. I'm not saying that fear isn't relevant today. If you stand on a cliff ready to jump, you'll be filled with fear. This is there to stop you from jumping. Fear today stops people when it's necessary. Once you have the skills you need to succeed, you'll find that only by pushing through your fears will you get the life you truly deserve.

HOW TO DEAL WITH FEAR - 3 step process:

1. Get Prepared

The message of fear is simply to get prepared. Something ahead of schedule is coming and you need to prepare for it so that you're ready to deal with it. If you're scared of public speaking, then get prepared and practice a lot until it gets better.

2. Build it up

If you're going to speak in front of 5,000 people I suggest you build it up by speaking to 10 first, then work your way up to speaking in front of much larger groups. If you don't build up your skill, your courage and then your fear will get you.

3. Gain confidence

By developing competence in the specific area, you will become confident in no time. Real competence comes from mastering your skill over a period of time. The 10,000 hour law is applicable here. When you practice something for a minimum of 10,000 hours you are thought to have mastered your skill.

You can apply this to any situation in your life. A common challenge that many entrepreneurs fear is doing and paying their end of year tax. I had a friend who used to live in fear of paying taxes for his business. He would worry all day, everyday about whether his business would survive. When letters would come through the post he would avoid opening them or reading them, and do whatever he could to not think about them. His thinking was that at the end of the year he would just hope that there would be enough money in the business account to pay the tax bill. He would throw away tax reminders throughout the year and hope they would miraculously go away.

So, I said to him, "What if you were to look at the letter, take note of the message from it. Which means, **get prepared** to pay your taxes. Surely it's better to know in advance if you can't pay your tax bill, as you'll have more time to get prepared and you'll know what you need to make your business work more effectively?" Make sure your product and services are selling well and whether another area in the business needs to be looked at.

Build up your ability to deal with paying the taxes by investing in new skills to handle making the business work more effectively so that you don't need to worry about if the business can pay it or not.

Then **build your confidence** up over a period of time knowing that once you continue to invest into your business skills, you'll be more capable of handling any problematic market conditions."

He took the message onboard, came to some of my live programs, invested in my mentor support program and turned the business around into a 7 figure business. It's funny, sometimes in life you'll meet people and the solution to their problem is right in front of them, yet they can't seem to access it because of a negative emotional block in some shape or form.

Quick Action Exercise:

What's the fear that is holding you back?

How can you overcome the fear knowing what you know now?

What can you do having overcome the fear now?

S - The Secret to earning money is to know it can always be made and there is no such thing as failure

The secret to money is to understand and believe that money can always be made in the economy today. If you resolve a problem and learn the right skills, you can make a lot of money and it's completely open to anyone. I don't care where you are from, what your background is, what colour you are, what gender you are, success and money can always be made. Health on the other hand is not genetic.

I believe that success and wealth is built by developing and implementing powerful habits. Successful people typically come from the quality of the environment that they are surrounded by, rather than them being blessed or genetically gifted. I believe in nurture over nature. This has been proven time and time again. So, this means that you my friend, no matter what you've done up to this point, if you're willing to invest more in yourself, you'll be able to get more out. It will take time, energy, money, however, it will be worth it in the end.

You must never be defeated by perceived failure, as it's just feedback to let you know you're not quite there yet. Being truly successful requires you to push through your boundaries. Take your perceived failure onboard and you'll become better at whatever you do and move forward. Notice I use the term perceived because it's our choice whether we focus on the upside or the downside.

Only as you get stronger will success and money come to you. Most people stick to what they know because the perceived failure is too much for them to handle. However, everything you have gone through this far, has brought you to this very moment in your life and as you move forward remember that there is no such thing as failure. It's just a feedback process to make you stronger and enable you to get better at whatever it is that you're doing. Refine your approach every time and you are guaranteed to get to where you want.

Take time to practice these new concepts around your belief structures, this will take time. By adopting this new way of thinking, as you embody these changes, over time you will notice life changing results around communication, you'll become more successful and happy.

Quick Action Exercise:

Which of the new beliefs are your favourite and how can you use it daily?

Which one do you need to work on to get more clarity and better understanding?

Financial Freedom SUCCESS Belief system ™.

S - **SERVE** others daily and you will earn a lot more.

U - **(U) YOU** are in control of your mind and only you will make yourself rich.

C - **COMMUNICATION** is the response you get. What you give is what you get.

C - **CASH** (money) does grow on trees.

E - Money is **EVERYWHERE** when you understand all business is a solution to a problem.

S - The **SIGNAL** under all negative emotion is the key to all change.

S - The **SECRET** to earning money is to know it can always be made and there is no such thing as failure.

Please remember to keep going back to part 1 of this book and making sure you're on the right path. The more you go through it, the more sense it will make, the more opportunities you'll attract, the more doors will begin to open for you. It's important that you're attracting the right things for you and the more time and effort you make, the clearer your goals will become.

CHAPTER 8

CRITICAL DECISIONS THAT MAKE OR BREAK YOUR FUTURE

MASTER THE SKILL OF DECISION MAKING

"Before you can become a millionaire, you must learn to think like one. You must learn how to motivate yourself to counter fear with courage. Making critical decisions about your career, business, investments and other resources conjures up fear, fear that is part of the process of becoming a financial success." Thomas J Stanley

One of the most common reasons for heart attacks today, is constant levels of extreme stress and job dissatisfaction. When it comes to choosing the right path for you and your future, your decision making process is vital for your ongoing health, wealth and fulfilment in life.

Bronnie Ware an Australian nurse spent several years working with and caring for elderly in the last 12 weeks of their lives. She documented their regrets in their last moments and noticed that over time, the same themes kept recurring with phenomenal clarity. One of the most sobering and heartfelt regrets they voiced, was the regret of not living by their truth. That is, not doing what was important and essential to them.

Achieving balance and fulfilment is dependent on making the right choices. Today many of us end up feeling overwhelmed and unsure what the correct choice for us is. I have a powerful decision making process that I use, across all areas of my professional and personal life to ensure that you get consistent results to drive yourself to your ideal future.

However, here's the thing to remember about making decisions. You make decisions from a logical space as well as an emotional space. You need a balanced combination of both these influencers whilst recognizing that there are many unconscious biases that also affect your decision making processes.

Understandably, decision-making is a process which requires an element of time. When you are faced with indecision, a decision which should save you time and enable you to move forward quickly, could prove costly, potentially locking you in a state of limbo for longer than necessary, sometimes even for years.

Your destiny is shaped by the decisions that you make on a daily basis. After studying decision making habits of many successful people, I noticed some common traits around their decision making processes. Most successful people evaluate situations and opportunities very quickly, make a decision and then work hard to make that decision right.

People who get stuck, tend to over evaluate everything before making even the smallest decision. This inability to make a decision, creates a loop of constant indecision, which prevents them from moving forward.

More often than not, they find comfort in saying to themselves, "I will wait to make the decision, when the time is right" however that is still a decision to avoid making the decision in the first place. This sends a message to the brain to say its ok to not make a decision and it's ok not to move forward. Therefore, they get stuck not moving forward.

If you were to consider time as a man made construct, then the future is merely a reflection of how you perceive time will be, the past is a reflection of how you perceive those events through your own lenses. If the future is your perception of what it will be like and your past is a reflection of what it was like, does it make sense that the only 'real' time you have is the present moment?

The present moment of **NOW** is where your decision-making must begin. If you get used to making present decisions based on certain criteria, then you will accelerate your growth and momentum forward, to create the life and wealth you deserve.

The NOW Decision Making Formula ™

N - NEVER

Never look back. Make decisions based on progression towards your goal, vision and purpose. Be careful not to get lost on the hyper specifics of the process, instead practice the skill of making decisions quickly and confidently.

I'm sure you have met someone or have a friend who finds it

difficult to make a simple decision such as deciding where to eat dinner with their partner, even when they are only offered 3 options. Having made a decision, they spend most of their time wishing that they had chosen a different option.

This triggers a more significant problem than most people realize, as it conditions the brain to register that no matter what choice is made, happiness or pleasure is not achieved. Although you may be thinking, "so what Ed, big deal, it's a small decision, can that really affect other things in my life?" I would say most definitely! The small decisions you make over a period of time creates a pattern, which your brain recognizes and uses when making the big decisions. If you can't make a small decision without talking yourself out of that decision, how are you ever going to make the bigger decisions that really influence your future?

So, you have to realize that all you have is this present moment and what is currently in front of you. Make a conscious decision and make it right. Not only this but ensure that you make the decision so that it serves you the most by considering the **7 KEY ELEMENTS OF WEALTH ™** at each stage.

Quick Action Exercise:

What decision are you actively avoiding or need to make right now?

Make a decision that will enable your progress forward.

O - ONLY

Only start with tasks that you find difficult. If you do what is difficult first, on a daily basis, you will knock out the challenges in your life very quickly making it simpler and a lot easier too. Most people unconsciously look for the easiest tasks to solve first, when their brain is actually in the strongest position to deal with the difficult tasks.

Most people distract themselves with daily chores like cleaning their house, emptying the dishwasher, cleaning their email inbox out, checking Facebook. This prevents them from realising the progress they would achieve if they applied that effort to mastering things they found difficult.

I believe there is one key action, that must be tackled head on daily, that will take you rapidly further forward. The Pareto principle also known as the 80/20 rule, the law of the vital few states that, for many events roughly 80 % of the results come from 20 % of the prime actions. Pareto was an economist who attended the university of Lausanne in 1896 and his work was sparked from noticing that approximately 80 % the land in Italy was owned by 20 % of the population.

The key to decision-making boils down to identifying what your key decisions and daily actions need to be, in order to get you 80 % of your results so that you achieve a greater amount in less time.

For example, a lot of my primary actions daily are making calls on the phone, building and nurturing client relationships. My daily admin tasks are all taken care of by my team and my primary goals are either creating more content, which will create more potential clients to interact with us as a company or by speaking or meeting with potential clients and pitching our services. I make sure that I'm very clear about what is to be my high priority action that will bring the best results quickly.

Here's another example of how I've applied the 80 % 20 % rule. The weather in the UK is pretty unpredictable, so we really look forward to summer and hot sunny days, which are rare. When the sun comes out, many people make the most of sunny days, spending hours in the sun, often to the point where they get sunburnt. Knowing that I wanted to catch some sun but wanted to be as productive as possible, I quickly realised that I could sit in the sun for 15-20 minutes without sunscreen and get the same results as my fellow students who would sit in the sun for hours.

Quick Action Exercise:

Write in your journal now or on a piece of paper what your 20 % daily actions are that will get you 80 % of your results? If you don't know right now, it's time to start considering what they are. Go back to the **Inner DRIVE system ™** to remind yourself of the key element you want to improve in The **7 Elements of Wealth™** Design the specific steps that you need to take right now to progress in that area starting now.

Now that you have decided what action you need to take, run it through this process to solidify it in your mind and give you the fuel to follow through.

4 step logical decision making formula

Ask yourself these 4 critical questions before making a decision:

1. What is the best case scenario from making this decision here now?

2. What is the worse case scenario from making this decision here now?

3. What it the most likely scenario from making this decision here now?

4. Countdown from 3 seconds and make the decision and follow through on it.

It's important to map out what is the best upside from making the decision, so you know that it's worth it, is also important to know the down side. Growing up with a brother as a lawyer he was always happy to remind me of the potential downside. When I was young I never really took the down side into play because I was always just focused on the potential benefit. As Warren Buffet says, only invest money into something that in the worse case scenario you are prepared to lose all of it. Then working out the most likely scenario gives you a fair approach to the possibility of what will happen, so you have the contrast between the best and the worst and the most likely.

It's time to make a decision and to stick to it and follow through. Most people again will say, I am not going to decide now. Which is still a decision. It's a decision to say I'm going to stay stuck where I am and not move forward. There is always a price to pay. There is a price to pay to moving forward, it's uncomfortable at times, there will be resources that are needed, money, time and energy are required to make it happen however, most overlook the price that you pay for staying the same and playing safe. As time goes by, it gets harder to make decisions and as one gets older, people tend to become more fear based and are less capable of moving forward through the fear.

Quick Action Exercise:

Get your journal ready and quickly think about the decision that you need to make in your life right now. What is it? Again align with the **Inner DRIVE system ™**. Focus on one of **THE 7 KEY ELEMENTS OF WEALTH ™** and ask yourself what is a hard decision that I need to make that will support me further, moving forward and progressing in this area.

1. What is the best case scenario you would get from making this decision **NOW**?

2. What is the worse case scenario you would get from making this decision **NOW**?

3. What is the most likely case scenario you would get from making this decision **NOW**?

4. Countdown from 3 seconds and make your decision **NOW**.

W - Create a WOW moment

The last piece is to create an emotion around what you are experiencing to help you become more empowered about moving forward. You may've run yourself through the above logical process and stopped at the end with maybe fear stopping you in some shape or form. Fear can be very disempowering and the only way to overcome it, is by creating a **WOW** moment so that you feel empowered enough to be able to make the decision.

In my consultancy, I take people through an active process so that they experience first hand what it's like to overcome a potential block and create an open frame in the brain. I then do some cognitive retraining, which allows a new discovery and learning or insight to dissolve the fear, leaving the person feeling super empowered and excited about moving their lives forward.

Some of the confronting challenges my team and clients overcome and experience include breaking through chunky pieces of wood, walking over hot coals, kayaking through rapids and jumping from incredibly high treetops. This allows them to experience a new empowered state and feeling of accomplishment.

Most people go through life not really understanding fear or being able to deal with fear which holds them back. Most people get stuck in an emotion and then label themselves as that experience. For example people who suffer with depression suffer for many years and have little or no idea of how to conquer it. Please give them a copy of this book to help them begin their journey to become more aware of themselves and the possibilities that are out there for them. I believe anyone can conquer depression with the right help and training once they understand the key concepts.

It is scientifically researched and proven that you can't be depressed whilst you are running.

Running won't solve all your problems however research shows that if you change your energy daily, the way you use your body, what you label your experiences as, the language you use, this will have a massive impact on the thoughts you have. If you focus on good things versus bad things, this will impact your feelings which will affect your body and the actions you take daily.

For years now, many have realised that the mind body connection is no longer just an abstract concept. There are thousands of studies on the placebo effect to prove how real this connection is.

For example in one study, researchers gave test candidates amphetamines (uppers) and told the then that they were given Benzodiazepines (downers). A high number of candidates in the case studies reported side effects of taking downers. They had slower heart rates, less energy, even though they had taken amphetamines which create the complete opposite result. The researchers then reversed the process and gave the test candidates Benzodiazepines (downers) and told them they had been given amphetamines (uppers). Again a high percentage of the patients reported side effects of the amphetamines (uppers). They had increased heart rates, rapid breathing and more energy even though they had taken downers. Your beliefs and thoughts are powerful and can have a direct affect on your physiology.

When you help someone overcome a bad experience in their life, they will believe it's possible to do anything. The brain starts to think, 'if I can do this, then what else can I do?' I had a very dear client who I helped overcome a range of challenges, one being, speaking in front of an audience. She came to all my live training programs and as a result, she completely overcame her fears. She ended up presenting to her boss, getting a raise, started a consultancy business on the side and went from strength to strength.

Quick Action Exercise:

Take a moment and break from what you're doing right now. Read this and then imagine I'm there with you and helping you, guiding you through an active visualisation, get your journal out so that you remember to document the process. I know you might be thinking this is stupid. Our mind creates fear countless times each day which means it's very good at it because it gets the opportunity to practice it repeatedly. It's easy for us to imagine ahead of schedule, something going wrong, not working out the way we want it to. When we do this regularly on a daily basis, it becomes second nature.

When you are scared of something coming your way, you worry about it. What your brain is doing is imagining it's real as if it's happening in the **NOW** and thus you are experiencing it in the **NOW**. If someone is scared of public speaking for example, they tend to project that fear ahead of schedule and even the thought of it, results in sweaty palms, tightened fists, a rapid heart rate.

Imagine if I called you up on stage with me in front of thousands of people. Imagine everyone staring at you, your heart is racing, you can sense your voice beginning to tremor, your hands are shaking, your palms are sweaty, you start worrying about what to say, what will people think, your stomach starts to turn in knots, you start to feel as if you're going to pass out.

You can't focus on a clear thought, your inner dialogue starts driving you wild, you want to scream to release the pressure that is building up inside your body and your head, all these blank faces staring at you waiting to hear you speak ....

I want you to notice your body and your feelings right now.

It's not actually happening is it? It's just a thought ahead of schedule and your body is feeling the effects in the now. What's amazing is the brain doesn't know the difference between what is real and what isn't real.

This time we're going to take the same process and use it for something more empowering. We're going to go back in time when you did something that you were proud of and practise feeling it in the now. This is a weaker experience than doing a real live experience. This is a recalled experience and we're asking our memory to go back to a time when we felt good. We are practising feeling good in the moment to raise our energy, raise our emotional state so that we can make an empowered decision, feel the fear and conquer it with our new empowered state.

I don't know what you'd be like on stage without any preparation, maybe you'd be ok, maybe you wouldn't. Regardless of how you'd respond, you'll notice quite clearly the difference you feel in your body imagining a stressful situation compared to one where you felt empowered. The good news is that it's all down to how you train your mind to behave to stimulus.

This comes from a real science background. It was first founded in the work of Twitmyer which was published in his doctoral dissertation in 1902 on the patella tendon reflex. Twitmyer did the first initial work on the stimulus reflex and what he noticed was when he hit a patient on the knee repeatedly, the action would get coded and become conditioned to a point. When the hammer wasn't used and a fake action was, the stimulus to the knee would react accordingly. He swapped the stimulus of the hammer and rang a bell and got the same effect. This became known as the stimulus response.

Ivan Pavlov was given a lot of the credit for the work even though it was Twitmyer who had paved the way. He tested a similar process of stimulus response with dogs. He trained dogs to eat at a certain time of day and rang a bell simultaneously. The dogs linked up eating and the bell together and they became neurologically woven together. Every time he rang the bell, the dogs came running and thought it was time to eat. Not only that but they were salivating in preparation for the food.

It's fair to say that our behaviour is nothing more than positive or negative experiences that have been hardwired into our neurology over time. Marketing agencies have used this for years. For example: whenever I asked people what their future looked like, they would say (depending on their age), "The future's bright, the future's orange." Orange was a large mobile phone provider that used to advertise before movies aired. Here's another one, "Just do it" you think of Nike, "I'm loving it" you guessed it Macdonalds. These slogans, the stimulus become hard wired in our experience. One of the major keys to finding wealth in your daily experiences is getting good at bringing back past, positive experiences into the present using this technique and allowing you to experience it in the present so that you can move forward into your future and conquer your potential challenges.

Quick action exercise:

Imagine a time in your past. Either close your eyes or keep them open whatever is easier for you. Take a moment now and imagine a time in your past when you broke through and felt proud. Imagine a specific time. Maybe you did something great, maybe you achieved something against the odds, and you didn't think it was possible. As you float back to that empowering moment notice what you see,

Notice what you hear

Notice what you feel

Notice what you were saying to yourself

Notice how you were breathing

Notice what your body was doing

See what you saw

Hear what you heard

Feel what you felt

Say the words that you said to yourself

Do the actions that you were doing

Think the thoughts that you were thinking

Notice again how you feel

Notice your breathing

Notice your actions

Notice your body

And when you're ready, come back into the room and notice yourself where you are now.

I appreciate that in this context it might be more difficult than if I was talking you through it. You can always visit my website and download some of my online training programs where I visually take you through guided processes. www.edjcsmith.com

You may have noticed that you felt good going through that process and the better you get at it, the more real you can make it. Like all things, negativity is trained over a period of time, through our education, background and experiences. Positivity is also trained over a period of time. The more you practice these techniques, the better you will become.

In order to get the wealth you deserve, you have to manage how much time you spend feeling good vs feeling bad daily. It's vital that you create consistent, positive habits daily that will empower you to create, be and do whatever you want to do.

CHAPTER 9

THE QUICKEST ROUTE TO PERSONAL WEALTH

FIND YOUR PASSION AND MAKE IT WORK FOR YOU

People who go through the traditional education system either leave school as soon as possible and get a job or they go on to study further, often accumulating a lot of debt along the way.

This is your life in a simplified diagram

THIS IS YOUR LIFE

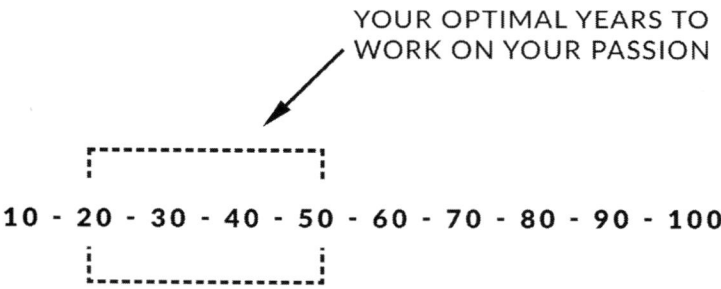

YOUR OPTIMAL YEARS TO WORK ON YOUR PASSION

10 - 20 - 30 - 40 - 50 - 60 - 70 - 80 - 90 - 100

Your adult life is when you are supposed to find happiness and fulfilment, earn some money, buy nice things, feel good and give back beyond yourself. This is what we intend to create when we are young and what we perceive to be a happy and fulfilled life, before retiring and enjoying free time. However, most people work their whole life until they retire and then maybe enjoy themselves if their health permits it.

The key is to ensure that you're working and doing something that you love at the same time. When your time is up, you are going to look back and regret that you didn't do more of the things you wanted to do. Please take a moment and pause before you read this next statement.

YOU ARE GOING TO DIE. YOU ARE NOT GETTING OUT OF LIFE ALIVE!

None of us are getting out of life alive. I want you to take action and create the life you really want. Work in and on your passion daily. If you can link it to generating money, even better because then you'll become a master and will be able to command a high fee for your time. Time is your most valuable commodity and using it wisely is the real secret to a happy balanced life. If you're really working in and on your passion, then you won't care how long it really takes.

Finding your passion

You have one life and it's better to live a short life that is filled with people and things that you love, than to live a long life that is filled with things that you don't like. The time to make the most of your life, is when you have health and the awareness to achieve great results, between the age of 22-50.

If you're spending time doing something that doesn't support your future growth, help you develop and become the best version of yourself, then it's time to make a decision, cut the cord and start on a new path that does serve you. There's a saying: 'If you want to capture the island, make the decision to do so, burn the boat to ensure that when you land on the island that there's no going back.'

Quick Action Exercise:

STEPS TO FINDING YOUR PASSION

1. What did you dream about when you were a child?

2. What were your hobbies then and what are they now?

3. What do you do for work?

4. What advice do you give to others?

5.   What would you do if money was not a problem?

6.   Is there something that you do when you don't ever look at the time?

7.   If you were to be a superhero, which character would you be and why?

HOW TO BEST SPEND YOUR TIME:

Your time is by far your most valuable asset. Many people believe that it is money, but it's not money. Money can always be made but time can't ever be replaced. People often say to me, 'What is the best environment to spend my time in and how can I get the most out of my time?' The more you learn, the more you will earn and if you create the most powerful environment for you and your family, then you'll have a more fulfilled life. Our lives are a by-product of who we spend time with, so it's essential that you really do spend as much time around people that are playing at a higher level than you.

THE KEY STAGES IN LIFE AND YOUR PRIORITIES

0 - 20 - Focus on passions, solid family values, experiences and lots of positive encouragement, reading, after school learning made fun.

20 - 30 - Focus on getting lots of experience, ideally working for a young company, build relationships and contact building. Work on social skills, business skills, entrepreneurship skills, mindset and motivation.

30 - 40 - Start something on your own or create joint ventures, start giving back beyond yourself.

Double down on what you have been planting the years before.

40 - 60 - Master your skills and leverage your business contacts, align for maximum potential.

60+ Reap what you have sowed, spend time deepening your relationships.

The past has gone, don't live there. Your happiness and success is defined by the way you live in the present moment. Take action, move forward and seize the day for today is a gift and tomorrow is not guaranteed. Your past might have failed you, but I won't.

CHAPTER 10

WHY SCHOOL FAILED YOU

HOW KNOWING THIS WILL
DEVELOP YOU

People often say to me, "I wish I learnt this at school, why didn't someone tell me this earlier on in life?" Traditional education only really prepares you for the early stages of adult life.

I realised from an early age, that there was a flaw in the system as I spent loads of time with entrepreneurs who had their own businesses. Why should we wait for retirement to feel happy and do the things we love? Surely, we can live a happy and fulfilled life now?

Let me show you a visual representation of what it really looks like (Picture of the job model).

JOB TO INVESTOR MODEL

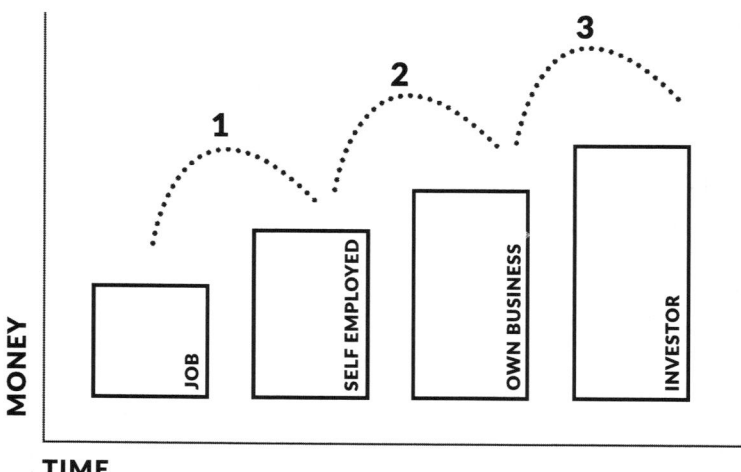

Stage 1: Getting a job

Most people go through education and then get funnelled into a job. How they end up in that job depends on a range of factors: they may have chosen that line of work because their parents advised them that it would be suitable, they believe it will get them where they want to be in 5 - 10 years' time. Perhaps the job works for them. It's near to where they grew up and it was the only choice they had. However, it comes about, they'll find themselves in a job working for someone else. Now it's fair to say at stage 1, this is where you're going to be paid the least amount of money and have the least amount of time.

Stage 2: Getting a better job

In the progression process of life, stage 2 is where you work your way up the ladder and get a better job. Your new role might include a new job title, more pay, more responsibility, more flexibility and training. More often than not, this position requires more of your time.

Stage 3: Start a passion project on the side

At stage 3, a person starts to look for other opportunities. Maybe they want more time, more money and have reached the ceiling in their current position? The individual starts looking at transitioning. They want to do something on the side of their current job. Something that they are inspired by and passionate about. Let's call it their "passion project".

Their passion project can be anything from a blog, a YouTube channel, a shopping store, an amazon store, a coaching business, providing services or products to a specific market.

Think of your "passion project" as a potential project. Do you remember presenting your end of year project to your class? Use this as a metaphor for your potential business moving forward. I think a lot of time people fail during their transition as they're not willing to change and adapt potential new projects.

The key drivers in stage 3 tend to be a burning desire to do what you're passionate about, want to earn more money and do something that inspires you and gets you jumping out of bed in the morning.

At stage 3, one of the biggest hurdles standing in the way is time and money. Most people struggle to keep up their job and their "passion project" on the side. This stage is very dangerous. Without the right support, people might give up their job too quickly. If their "passion project" fails, they might end up having to return to a job.

Stage 4: Working full-time in your passion project

Now this is the ideal situation for a lot of people. Working full time in something that they truly love, earn great money and are successful and happy. However, the reality is that more often than not, people have even less time than before because they are working every hour that God sends. The biggest challenge at this stage is cash flow.

Stage 5: Becoming a business owner

You only become a true business owner once you can step away from it and the business is able to operate on its own. At stage 5 if done correctly, this will free up a lot of your time, as the business is able to run without you being there.

Stage 6: You become an investor

This is where it's at! You'll have the most time and money and be able to invest into other businesses.

This is where the likes of Richard Branson end up on their island working from a hammock. He has over 400 different business that operate without him there. This is where you make the greatest impact in the world and take it to a new level. By leveraging your money, you create more money, have the most amount of time to do the things that you want. The key is to become an investor as quickly as possible.

Quick Action Exercise:

Where are you right now?

What is your challenge to get to the next stage?

How can you resolve it now?

How you transition through the stages effectively is by understanding the 3 key stages to income generation and I am going to cover that in the following chapter.

CHAPTER 11

GENERATE 3 SOURCES OF INCOME TO SECURE YOUR FREEDOM

LEVERAGE YOUR TIME

Money won't buy you happiness, but it sure helps!

I know what it's like to have money and not have money. I believe you can create more good in the world today with money than you can ever create without it. When I read Richard Branson's biography, he explained that people still send him hate mail and negativity about his wealth today, even though he's given so much to charity and created so much for mankind. The problem is people are jealous of other people's successes. Once you become more successful, you'll soon find out who your real friends are.

There are 3 sources of income that you need to master:

1. Active Income

Active income is produced from your job. The more skills you have, the more active income you'll earn. Please note, you don't get paid per hour. A lot of people think they get paid per hour. Think about that for a moment. You get paid by the value you provide in that hour. When you upgrade your skills, you get paid more per hour. A general practitioner (GP) who works in the local doctors' surgery gets paid less than the Specialist who is a brain surgeon who works in Harley Street in central London. The key to increasing your active income is to update your skills and continue to do this as you go through your career.

Having one income stream today is not enough due to the unpredictable economy. It's far safer having multiple streams so that you're not reliant on only one stream.

A lot of people start weighing up their hourly rate against everything they do. Earning an hourly rate can hold you a slave to your hours as you begin to weigh up missing your hourly rate versus doing something else. The only way you break this cycle is learn a new skill set. Although you might initially lose in the beginning, in the long run your new skill will enable you to charge more per hour in the future.

Quick Action Exercise:

How can you now work on improving your active income?

What skills could you learn to take your hourly rate up?

2. Passive Income

The second major income stream you need to build is your passive income. This is where you start putting your effort into your "side line project" and over a period of time, it starts to generate income for you. You must manage it, spend time building up your skill set. Set up multiple streams of income that will enable a passive stream of income to build up. This will allow you to free up your time and transition into your full time business. When you have passive income coming in, you can literally buy back your time because you have an income generator working for you. The key here is to look after your passive income streams, making sure they are stable and lucrative whilst you keep investing in your skills.

Quick Action Exercise:

Do you have a passive income stream?

If not, why not?

Can you learn to monetise your passion?

3. Leveraged Income

The last source of income is when you leverage your income to buy other businesses that become income generators for you. At this stage, you will get the most amount of time back if you manage it properly and have the potential to make the most amount of money. Again, these are not guaranteed, and it doesn't come without risk. One of the best ways to start thinking of yourself as an investor is by spending time with people that invest rather than consume. If you were to spend $300 in 2004 into Apple as an investor rather than as a consumer, your investment today would be in the millions. Who you spend time with is who you become.

Quick Action Exercise:

What skills can you invest in, so you can increase your earning potential?

If you have £5,000 and left it in the bank for 6 years, with inflation you would actually get less out than you originally invested.

If you invest £5,000 into your mind and business skills, how much more could you charge because of those skills? You would end up earning more in the long term.

I teach people to become coaches, consultants and leverage their skills. With these skills, once people realise their earning potential in the market, it becomes a no brainer decision to invest with me.

CHAPTER 12

LEARN TO PUNCH ABOVE YOUR WEIGHT AND RUN WITH THE BIG DOGS

YOUR NETWORK = YOUR NET WORTH

One of the significant ways I changed my decision making processes and earning more, was by spending time with people who were way ahead of me, who already had their own businesses and were living the life I dreamt of. If you spend time with people who are ahead of you, you'll make conscious decisions that are out of your current thinking patterns and capabilities.

In order to acquire more wealth and make the right decisions that will get you there, you need to spend time with people that are ahead of you and more advanced than your current thinking. This will enable you to see your challenges from a different perspective, allowing you to move forward more quickly and successfully.

I invested heavily into my education in 2001. I read a range of books that really changed my thinking. A business client of mine at the time had given me a book and told me to read it and go and meet the character in the book. I tracked him down, booked a session with him and paid him £10,000 for 2 hours of his time. At the time my friends thought I was crazy. I was too scared to tell anyone, so I kept it very quiet.

After my session, I joined his other programs and invested another £10,000. I flew back thinking, "how the hell am I going to explain that I've just spent £20,000 on my education?" Because I had invested such a large amount in my education, my drive and commitment increased, I noticed my life and business changed significantly. Up to that point I was doing very well. I was earning a solid, consistent income in my first business venture and I was building my buffers with other businesses, securing my safety and stability. I started to realise the power of who you spend time with is who you become. After the sessions, I started to realise that if I could spend time with people who were earning a lot more than me, then I could pick their brains and could save myself a lot of time by learning from their success.

As I started believing more in myself, I started pitching my services to private clinics in Harley Street and Wimpole Street, some of the most prestigious streets in central London. It took me 7 months to secure a private room in Wimpole Street. Some of the A list celebrities that visited the clinic at the time included Princess Diana, Michael Jackson, Gwyneth Paltrow.

An incredible thing happened. Because of my move to Wimpole Street and my association, I was able to charge a lot more for my services. I charged more per hour and got better results. It was crazy. By making these changes, I went from hustling people for my services to earning great money, serving extremely satisfied clients who had better results, all because I made the simple decision to invest in myself, commit and follow through.

If you hang around people who are unhappy and negative, you will more than likely be unhappy and negative too. However, if you hang around friends who are supportive and focus on the positive, the chances are you'll be supportive and focused too.

Quick Action Exercise:

Who's ahead of you that you can invite to meet up for a drink and a chat? Who can you ask to meet for lunch and discover what their crucial decisions were that enabled them to get where they are today?

Who can you send an email to and find out what decisions they wish they'd avoided making? Whose event would you like to attend next?

Whose book can you read next?

Whose audio program can you download next?

Whose online program can you go through next?

Rapidly speed up your decision making process by getting a mentor

Get yourself a mentor to help you make the right decisions and hold you accountable. Making the right decisions today are so important because it literally can shave off years or add years to your journey if you get it wrong. If you don't know how to scale your business and have no idea how to drive traffic through social media, you are missing a trick today.

For many years I've invested into getting people on board to help me move further forward. At different stages of my journey, I've invested into many different mentors who have really sped up my levels of success in different areas. Here are some resourceful ways you can get people on board to help you.

When picking someone to help you

1. Pick someone based on their results if you want similar results too.

2. Are they going to be able to nurture you and be aligned with your personal goals?

3. Are they a good communicator? It's no good if they're unable to understand where you are and what your challenges are.

4. Are they a happy, fulfilled person? This is very important. Never learn from anyone that is unhappy and not fulfilled in what they do because this might be the result you get too.

I would always recommend that you pay someone for their time. If they have something to offer and it has great value, then it's worth the investment. All business greats leverage their time very effectively. If you want to sit down with Warren Buffet it will cost you around 1 million pounds and you will be in a group with 30 other people. If you want to hire Richard Branson to speak at your event, it will cost you £500,000 and all the money will go to his charity. At this stage, I charge my personal time out for keynote speaking events between £10,000 - £20,000 depending on who I'm speaking to and what the opportunity is.

If you want an investor to invest in your business and become your mentor, then you have to be prepared to offer a juicy business deal, so that they benefit from the joint venture otherwise, there's nothing in it for them and it won't be worth their time.

CHAPTER 13

CLIMB THE CAREER LADDER
WITHOUT RISKING YOUR LIFE

FEEL BETTER ABOUT YOUR
BUSINESS

The Rules of the new economy is not about getting it's about giving. If you're not prepared to give more than your competition, then it will be very hard for your business to really stand out and get the traction needed. The reason why people don't succeed in their passion project with the shift from having a job into their own business comes down to these principles.

Reasons why you fail to progress

1. You don't give enough

They don't give enough to the process. They don't give enough to take on more clients. They don't give enough to those clients when they do come on board. Giving is not about hoping that because you've given to your client first, the law of reciprocation will kick in and that person will automatically give back to you. If you're not aware of the unconscious law of reciprocation, the law states that we are hardwired to want to give back to someone that has already given to us because it's hardwired in our psyche. If you wave at someone they will usually wave back. Maybe you've been caught in the crossfire of someone else waving, you thought they were waving at you, you look around and realise that in fact they were actually waving at someone behind you. It's too late your hand went up and you reciprocated, even though you didn't know the person.

Providing a great service or product is about wanting the other person to experience something world class, something they value and want to tell their friends about because they are blown away with the high level of care they received. Some people don't give enough of their time to the process and aren't passionate about either the service or product they provide. They don't invest their own money into the process and are held back because of their money fears. The only way to create a passion project is to keep investing in your skill set until you reach the tipping point and the income is generated because of the skills that you have learnt.

2. You're in the wrong environment

I don't care how strong or positive you think you are, if your environment doesn't support your growth, you won't get to where you want to be.

If you spend too much time with people who don't support your transition, then the transition will simply not happen. If all of your friends work in a safe job, then you will more than likely go back to your safe job. I can't stress enough that the transition journey needs to be supported and nurtured. Our academy provides a lot of support to our students, a lot more than most other providers because we know how vulnerable people are, being surrounded by the right people is when they go through this transition period.

3. You have the wrong mentor

Unfortunately, in today's market there are a lot of people who sell the shovels having never actually done any digging themselves. Getting the right sort of mentor as a guide is essential. I strongly recommend that you take time and care when choosing one. A lot of the corporate consultancy work that we attract, is based on my long standing reputation in the industry and my open transparency for what we can and can't deliver. Today we compete for many of the top accounts and I put this down to staying humble and grounded. When choosing a mentor, it's imperative that you have open and honest conversations early on in your relationship so that everything is transparent.

4. Your business doesn't solve a big enough problem

Business is all about finding a problem and resolving it. If your passion project doesn't resolve a problem for someone, then there's no point doing it because you won't earn enough to leave your full time job. Taking time to work on your passion project and learning to monetise from it, is an essential step.

Today almost everything can be monetised if you are willing to put enough time and finances into it.

5. The opening offer (to get to know, like and trust you) is not good enough

In today's market you have to be prepared to give more than anyone else. If you're not willing to give a high value offer open gift of some sort to entice new customers, then you will be eliminated from the market. You can't compare yourself to strong brand businesses that have been in the market for a long time that have a higher brand presence already. You have to be willing to give a great quality product or service that is a taster offer, to get people into your business otherwise, you will never generate a happy, client base and you will have to go back to your job. If you're not prepared to give and do more in your role, you will be replaced by someone else who is.

You must make a decision to commit to giving and serving others more than anyone else in the market with the quality of your product, the experience and customer support. The greatest decisions you will ever make is found daily in your **Reality Creator** ™ which we will cover on the next chapter.

CHAPTER 14

DECIDE WHAT YOUR DESTINY IS

GET WHAT YOU WANT

Everyday people wake up and have minor decisions to make. Many are completely unaware and unconscious of the powerful decisions they need to make in order to shape their destiny, however most believe that they are.

Many people focus on decisions like:

Should I leave my job or start a new job?

Should I start something on the side?

Can I start something on the side?

Should I give up or keep pushing through with my business?

Am I on the right path?

What is the purpose of my life?

Now I am not implying that these are not important decisions. However, with little guidance, you'll see that there is one decision that you need to make. Once you become aware of the ultimate decision, you will be able to create anything in your life. There is nothing you won't be able to do.

What is the ultimate decision that you need to make?

REALITY CREATOR

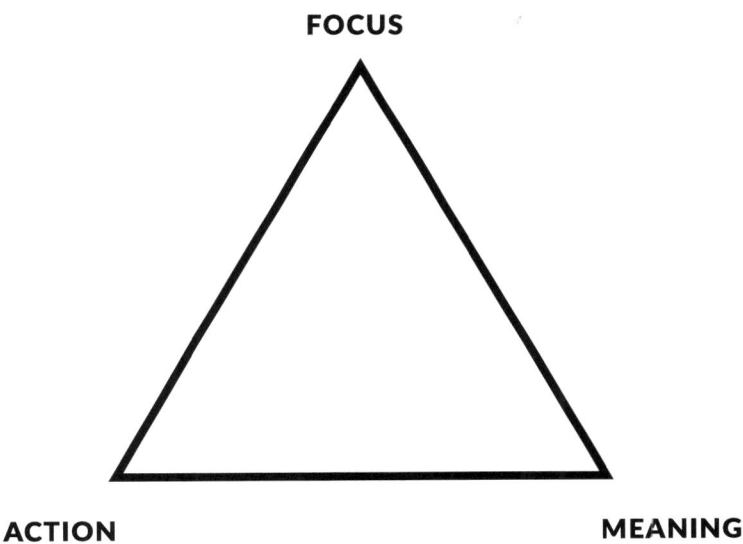

FOCUS

ACTION   MEANING

Mastering Your Reality Creator So You Can Get What You Want

Your reality is created by what you focus on. The meaning you give to things and therefore the action you take because of it is all created by what you choose to focus on. It never stops, it's always operating within you and ultimately it will define what sort of reality you create.

The major factors that influence this initially are:

1. Your background

2. Your past experiences

3. Your current education

4. Your parenting

5. Who you spend time with on a consistent basis

Let me give you some practical examples. Your reality is defined by what you focus on. Every day you have an opportunity to focus on all the good things in your life versus all the bad things that have happened in the past. For the most part, you are completely unaware of your current trained focus. If you focus on the good things then more good things will come to you, if you focus on the bad things then more bad things will start to happen.

What's wrong in life is always easy to notice however, what's right is equally easy when you train yourself to notice it. Your default settings have been influenced by the 5 key factors outlined above and these ultimately define your response to every situation you encounter. Whether you find an empowering focus and label the experience with a powerful meaning that serves, strengthens and helps you move forward or the complete opposite which is limiting and disempowering, is all down to what you focus on.

Let's take a simple phrase someone might say to you - **"You should get a better job"**

Focus on the negative:

When considering that statement from a negative point of view, you may feel that it reflects directly on you. For instance you may feel that your efforts and therefore you, aren't good enough. Or you'll feel maybe that your job is unattractive and therefore you are unattractive. It may even be as simple as you believing that your friend is better than you, that you are lazy and you should do better. Nonetheless, by seeing the phrase as a disempowering phrase, you are likely to be resentful towards your friend, resentful to taking positive action, as well as to your friendship in general.

Focus on the positive:

However, when considering the statement from a positive point of view, you may feel a sense of pride, that you are too good for your job, that you should be appreciated more, that you are better than what you are currently doing because you have so much potential. Not only does hearing this make you feel so much better about yourself, but you hold your friend in higher regard as well. That's a good friend who obviously cares enough to say something to you because they want to see you progress and help you move forward. By labelling the experience as a good experience, you take positive action towards getting that better job and your friendship grows deeper and stronger.

Notice how these two scenarios create very different paths in your life. If you focus on the negative, then you end up in a very different situation than if you focus on the positive. That was one simple phrase. Imagine all the times you've been unaware of focusing on the positive. The problem here is that a lot of people walk around with the mask of positivity on when underneath they've been trained to focus on all the bad things happening around them. People in the UK are renowned for being negative and walking around pretending that everything is ok when it's clearly not.

I encourage you to take this simple example and look at it on a deeper level. If you want more results in your life, it's time to question yourself. Do you focus on the good things happening to you and do you really find the good in all the challenges that are sent your way? Or do you focus on the bad?

It's only under stress that you find out what someone's habitual hard wiring is. We can all focus on the good, when everything in our lives is going well, we've food on our table and we're feeling really good.

What's it like when you are under stress? That is the key barometer, that is the difference as to whether you'll be hugely successful or not. If you can't find the good when you're facing the bad times in your life, then you'll give up and stop moving forward.

An inspirational example is the story of Nelson Mandela. On being released from prison, he was asked, "what was it like being enslaved?" He replied, "I wasn't enslaved, it was my choice to stay there, I was getting prepared for my mission." He instantly changed the meaning of the statement by changing the focus.

He changed the focus from being 'enslaved' to 'getting prepared', which is so powerful. This allowed him to continue getting stronger whilst he was in prison because every year he was given a choice to walk free only if he gave up his mission and went back to how it was before. He refused and therefore changed the meaning of the statement. If he hadn't done that, then he would never have made the 27 years of positive personal improvement and would've given up his mission. Become more aware of what you're focusing on, the good things in your life vs the bad things and especially when you're stressed.

Here's another great illustration I teach my students. There was an old story that went a little bit like this.

An old, wise man lived on a farm. He had one horse that would plough his fields for vegetables. One day he woke up and the horse had run away. His neighbours said to him, "how are you going to feed your family without the horse? This must be the worst day of your life?"

He replied: Maybe

He'd been saving up vegetables in the house and was about to run out when he woke up one morning and realised that the horse had come back with six more horses. He now had 7 horses. His neighbours said, "wow this must be the best day of your life, now you can increase your food and start a business selling the vegetables, this must be the best day of your life?"

He replied: Maybe

The farmer had a beloved son. The son took advantage of the situation and set about getting the horses to work more so he could expand the family business and provide more food for the family. Unfortunately, whilst training the horses, he fell off a horse and broke his back. He was unable to walk again. The neighbours said to the farmer, "you must be so sad, this must be the worst day of your life?"

He replied: Maybe

As the months went past, a civil war broke out and all the sons in the local villages were rounded up and taken to battle. Fortunately, because the farmer's son couldn't walk, he was allowed to stay at home, help his father out and his life was spared. His neighbours said, "you're so lucky that you were able to keep your son at home, we had to part with ours. This must be the best day of your life?"

He replied: Maybe

Your life is quite simple. What you Focus on, what Meaning you choose to give it, is what Action you take from it.

Quick Action Exercise:

When something bad happens to you, force yourself to focus on the good things rather than the bad things. Can you notice the good things in any situation?

What happened to you in the past that was bad?

Can you find something good from it?

The more you practise this as a concept the stronger you will become.

THE REALITY CREATOR ™ is internally coupled together with **THE REALITY FUEL GENERATOR ™**

These are powerful individually but rely on each working effectively together for you to see results.

REALITY FUEL

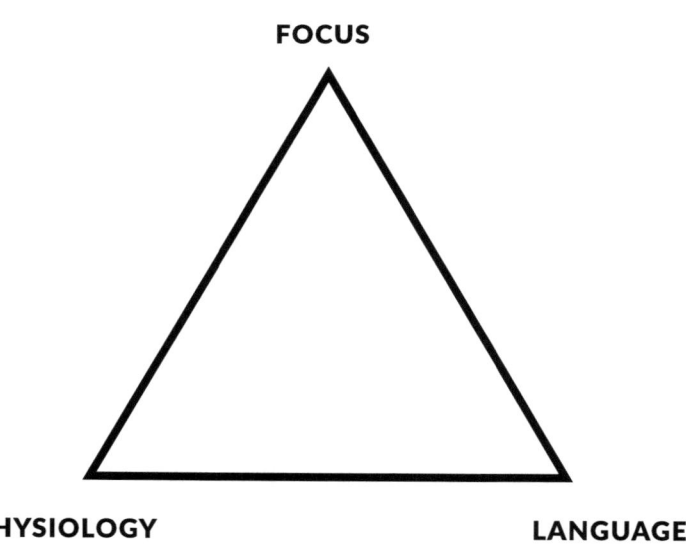

FOCUS

PHYSIOLOGY

LANGUAGE

Again I want to reiterate that what you focus on is key to everything you achieve. The same principles apply here as they did in the Reality Creator. What you choose to label the experience as and what meaning that you choose to give it, comes from the language that you use. The action you take once you have gone through this process depends on what happens in your body at the same time or shortly after.

The language you use when giving an experience meaning is incredibly important to be mindful of. If you choose empowering language when you're going through tough challenges, you'll have a different feeling inside of you, compared to when you label an experience with disempowering language, you'll find the experience very different.

Therefore your focus, the meaning you give an experience and how this affects your body, it will affect the action you do or don't take. Can you see how all these elements are so intrinsically linked and how powerful you will be once you have mastered them?

Example:

You get up earlier than normal - Negative Focus = how tired you are because of it.

You say "I'm tired"

Action: your brain & body then find all the ways in which to make you feel tired.

You get up earlier than normal - Positive focus = How much more energy you need to get more stuff done and stay alert.

You say " I need more energy"

Action: Your brain and body find ways in which more energy will come your way.

What you say to yourself labels the experience you have.

The key to changing your life and taking your mindfulness to a completely different level is to become aware of what you say every day and choose the most empowering words you can possibly experience. At the end of the day, who is in control of your brain? You are. How you handle it, is up to you.

Quick Action Exercise:

Now this is a short introduction into the power of language and how it can change your life.

As soon as you notice yourself saying something that disempowers you, stop saying those words. Quickly change the words to something more empowering and notice how this will in turn change your experience inside yourself.

Physiology

Your physical reaction (physiology) will influence what meaning you give an experience, the language you use whilst experiencing it and the action you take because of it. It's well documented that the mind and body are connected together through neurotransmitters. This is the liquid that covers your entire cells and allows the stimulus from the brain to connect to every fibre of your body.

The quickest way to change how you feel emotionally is to change your body posture. You may have read that communication is not all about what you say but what your body is saying too.

There are many studies that have divided communication into three different forms of which 7 % is attributed to the words you use, 35 % is attributed to tonality you use, 55 % is attributed to your body language.

It's easy to see that the most significant form of communication is your body language. It has been proven that you can't be depressed whilst running. If you're feeling depressed right now and don't believe me, go outside and run. Then notice how your body feels afterwards.

It's important to be mindful of how your physical state influences your mood or outlook on life as it's so quick and easy to change. The key to keeping your mood positive is to train your body and your mind simultaneously as they work together.

Whilst there are many studies you can look at, it really isn't rocket science. When you think of happy times in your life and you think of your body, how it felt, how you walked, held your head high, it's simple to see the connection.

If you're a footie fan you might say, " It was when my team won a football match and I was so happy and excited that I ran around the living room, punching the air and screaming at the top of my voice." Take a moment and relive that experience as though you were experiencing it for the first time. Notice what happens to your body. It feels great! Life feels great! You feel invincible!

If you wanted to feel that same experience again, you could replicate an intense level of happiness and excitement by replicating the behaviours of that experience by punching the air and screaming. You could relive that moment and remember the same picture you saw, you could remember exactly what you were saying, you could remember how you said it and the experience would represent itself inside of you.

Think about how good you would feel if you did that frequently. A recalled memory of the event will feel less potent than the actual event. However, by reliving that positive experience frequently, you'll find it easier to remember more details and create that state of extreme excitement and happiness more easily, almost effortlessly with practice.

The same is true if you relive negative or sad experiences frequently. If you can, imagine someone you know who has been or is sad and low. Consider their posture like how they hang their head, hold their hands and face down. You may have noticed them with slumped shoulders and hunched over sitting on a chair?

If you walked into a room and saw someone like this, you would typically expect that person to be sad or going through some tough times. You may even get a sense that they are mulling over something sad and saying things to themselves that are disempowering. They may be focusing on how they have messed up, what they did wrong and how awful they feel.

I want you to consider how quickly things would change if that person were to shift their focus from the negative and focus on what they had learnt instead and change their language so that it's positive and empowering. How would they feel if they decided to go running and whilst they were running shout to themselves, 'Every day in every way, I am getting stronger and stronger and stronger?' It would be impossible to stay sad or down, they would feel better about themselves and take positive action to move forward.

With training, re-education and consistent practice of refocusing to find the positives, everyone could change the affect their past has on their present and future. I've coached thousands of people and I can tell you that no matter what you have been through, no matter how hard it's been, I promise you, that you can heal from the pain and create a new future, just the way you want it.

The reason I do a routine every morning is that over a period of time, just like your body, your mind will begin to pick up the same positive experience. By starting your day like this, you are preparing yourself to become better equipped to handle the challenges in your life and complete the tasks that need to be done to achieve your goals.

Quick Action Exercise:

The next time you are feeling sad or lonely go for a run and notice how you feel afterwards.

Of course you might say, 'I don't want to, I don't feel like it.' Sometimes in life if you don't feel like doing something, then that's exactly what you must do. I know that if you focus on the good feelings that you will get after you've completed the exercise, you'll be very grateful you did it.

Where should I start?

You can see that all three factors, namely your focus, language and physiology are important so it's good to change all three. However, you can change these in order to start changing your life and getting better results.

By changing these, you will become the centre of your reality and the creator of all the good things in your life. With these skills, you can find new ways of dealing with challenges and letting go of the past, allowing you to create more of an empowering future for you and your family.

Change Your Focus, Choose an empowering focus to Change your life

You can change your focus on a daily basis and you'll start to realise how often this is going on in your life.

Change Your Language, Choose meanings that empower you to Change your Life

You can change the language you use daily so that you only choose empowered meanings to any situation. When you find yourself saying bad things to yourself, see if you can soften the words. What you say to yourself repeatedly is what you'll become so only say words of kindness and encouragement to yourself and others.

Change Your Physiology - Choose empowering actions to Change Your life

Every time you find yourself feeling low in energy or have a negative feeling, you can instantly change your posture. You can control your breathing, increase your energy by jumping up and down on the spot. I guarantee you this will raise your mood, directly influence your ability to take action, move forward and get the positive, happy hormones dopamine etc to allow you to feel good.

Start going out daily and nurturing successful habits.

If you would like a daily video to help build this habit, then please join **THE 7 KEY ELEMENTS OF WEALTH** ™ and I will send you a video every morning to help you take more action and get more results in the seven most important key areas of your life.

It's time to look at how we can attain the things that you want in life. In part 3 we look at attaining your results, keeping the success and how to ensure that you follow through on your commitments and make it happen. This is the most important section of the book and the part where so many people get it wrong and give up.

It's one thing to decide what you want, it's important to be able to make some decisions however, it's a completely different ball game to make sure that you follow through on your actions and secure the things you really want. So, let's get really super clear in part 3.

CHAPTER 15

ACTIONS TO ATTAIN LONG TERM WEALTH

MAKE IT HAPPEN

"Don't judge each day by the harvest you reap but by the seeds you plant" Robert Louis Stevenson

Attaining long term wealth and following through with your actions is the most important step in the book. I want to say thank you for getting this far as most people today rarely finish what they start. If you are reading this, well done for sticking to it and I want you to know, if you don't apply the last step then, what has come before this will be absolutely useless to you.

Committing and following through on your commitments is a never ending self-development process that must be managed. Like a baby, you have to keep nurturing it through their stages of growth. At the early stages of formulation, if you were to leave the child before they were ready to stand by themselves, they would regress and more than likely fail before their coping mechanisms were ingrained for them to continue on their journey and grow.

The accountability process is the most important part of the system because it's all very well having the motivation to get started, it's another thing to make the right decisions. It's a completely different skill to follow through and to actually turn your thoughts into actions and achieve new results.

Most people in life say one thing and then do a completely different thing. I'm sure you've had friends in your life who say they are going to do something and yet time and time again, do something else and don't follow through. Unfortunately, in today's society, a lot of people talk a good game yet when it comes to implementing and following through, they lack commitment.

In order for me to help you follow through on your commitments, I will take you through my accountability format **The Make It HAPPEN Model ™**

The Make It HAPPEN Model ™

H - How much are you willing to commit to making this idea, concept that you've been working on a reality?

1. How much money are you willing to invest into yourself and your idea?

You'll have to put some skin in the game if you want to get a good return on your investment at the end of the day. Standard Dragon Den's principles state that anyone who is going to invest into your ideas will want to know how much you've already invested into the project yourself. Have a clear amount of money that you're willing to invest into your potential idea, your growth and your business.

People often say to me, "Ed I want to earn a certain amount of money this year." It's good to be ambitious. However, if you want to earn £100,000 - £1,000,000 a year for example, the question is how much are you willing to invest in yourself to earn that amount of money? If you're sick of your current earnings, then you will have to change something to allow yourself to earn more, otherwise you will continue earning the same amount year after year.

2: How much time are you willing to invest into your project?

There will have to be a sacrifice in order for you to move forward. I'm afraid you can't watch every series on Netflix and expect to get great results. Get clear on your time scheduling. What I recommend is that you allocate and block time out each day to make sure that individual tasks are completed. For example, I allow a minimum of 1 hour for health daily. Then the rest of the day is split up into units of time. I don't have any meetings before 2pm in general and I do my best to delegate and make sure that where possible, someone other than myself, goes to meetings, unless they are really important.

Quick Action Exercise:

Write in your journal and commit an amount of money you are willing to invest in yourself.

How much time can you spend on following through on your actions?

A - At what date will this happen?

Most people avoid putting a date to aim for because it puts pressure on them. That is exactly the point of putting a date in the diary. Without the pressure to perform, human motivation dwindles rapidly. You need a date to aim for. Without a deadline it's normal for human motivation to die. On a more simplistic level, even the most unmotivated people have experienced this in some shape or form. When it comes to booking a holiday, something fascinating happens.

After people have completed their detailed research for their holiday, they pay their deposit and commit by booking in advance. They start to visualize themselves on the beach and imagine how wonderful their holiday is going to be. The day arrives, most people find they wake up before their alarm clock goes off on the day of their flight. As if their minds knew exactly what time to get up. Why then in the past, have they struggled to get up on time?

The reason for this is because this is exactly what's happened in your mind. Because the mind has been focused, there has been a financial commitment, they have spent a long time looking forward to the specific date whilst all that time the brain has been getting ready, is alive and raring to go.

If there is a date set, then the mind has something to aim for. An important factor to note here is that even if the goal is not achieved by that date, it doesn't matter because it has served its purpose. By setting a date you will experience a greater drive and sense of determination to achieve your goal because you have put it in your diary.

Quick Action Exercise:

Write in your journal and pick a date now when you will make this vision happen and stick to it. Put a date in your diary and aim for it.

P - People who are going to hold you accountable to make it happen

If you don't have someone hold you accountable to take action, it will more than likely not happen in the first place. Consider why Olympic athletes typically achieve their best time at their home ground, when all of their loved ones and family are watching them? It's because it creates a level of pressure and focus on the athlete, which is not achieved by internal motivation alone.

Consider why professional sports players and successful business people have coaches? So that they can achieve a higher level of productivity to guarantee that they make it happen on a daily basis. I would be very happy to hold you accountable, maybe in one of my online groups or in person if we ever get the chance to meet? Either way, it doesn't have to be me, get someone in your life who can hold you accountable to make sure you deliver on the things that you say you are going to do.

Quick Action Exercise:

In your journal decide who you can get on board to help you move further forward. Find someone who is ahead of you and ideally pay them, so they are invested into the process too. There's no point getting someone who is the same level as you already are, because you won't be pushed enough to achieve the goals you want to achieve.

If you would like me to hold you accountable personally, I have a range of options for you to choose from. See the **WHAT'S NEXT** section at the end of the book.

P - How much Profit do you want to make?

Quite simply decide how much do you want to earn? Pick a number that you can aim towards and go for it. How much is this going to be worth to you?

It's no good just working out the turnover. You need to know how much profit is left on the table. Many people get stuck when learning new skills because they don't realise how much more that skill will enable them to earn in the long term. I personally had trouble in this area. In the early years of my business career, I was stuck on an hourly rate and had to shift my thinking. I had to cut down my hours, where I would lose potential paid hours to learn new skills that would pay me more in the future.

Quick Action Exercise:

Write down exactly how much profit you want to make one year from now.

In order for you to make that sum of money, remember how much are you willing to commit to investing into yourself to make that a reality?

E - Envision - Envision it happening and prepare your mind to recognise what it will look like

To make your goal more real, consider what it feels like once you have achieved it. Visualise the outcome so that your brain starts to hardwire the actual experience as though it is a real experience that is already happening. This is so essential, there are so many documented experiments of the power of visualisation and how this helps steer you into creating the very thing you thought impossible. You should include as many details as you are able to, in order to make it as real and vivid as possible. The more you visualise it, the more real it will feel. Keep practising and over time it will become what you want to achieve. It will become clearer and your mindset will become stronger and stronger.

Quick Action Exercise:

Commit to visualising achieving your goals every day. Start with a minimum of 3 mins a day, whilst doing your morning ritual. This can easily fit into a 10 min slot in the morning.

Notice what you can hear? Whose voice can you hear? What are they saying to you? What are you saying to them?

Notice also what it feels like and what emotions you are feeling? What emotions are others around you feeling? How are you breathing? What happens now that you have achieved this? What more are you able to do now that you have done this?

N - Envision it not happening

Follow the same process as above but this time spend time seeing it not happening. The reason for this is because it will drive you further forward and will be an effective, motivating factor to ensure that you follow through. This should create an uncomfortable feeling, which in turn becomes a driving force inside you. It's vital to make sure that you associate deeply to your pain of not achieving your goal. Again, make it as real and painful as possible so that you create a higher amount of emotion inside you. How will you feel about yourself? How will others feel about you? What will you say to yourself? What will others say to or about you if you don't follow through?

Quick Action Exercise:

Commit to visualising you not achieving your goal. Start with a minimum of 3 mins a day, whilst doing your morning ritual. This can easily fit into a 10 min slot in the morning.

Notice what you can hear when you don't achieve your goal? Whose voice can you hear? What are they saying to you? Who have you let down? What are you saying to them? Notice also what it feels like and what emotions you are feeling. What emotions are others around you feeling? How are you breathing? Because you haven't achieved what you said you were going to, what has happened?

After finishing your visualisation of it not happening, make sure you clear your mind and focus on the good vision again. It's vital to finish this process focusing on the good happening. Now you can repeat the E - Envision it happening to make sure that you maintain a positive upbeat state.

CHAPTER 16

FIVE FATEFUL PITFALLS
MOST PEOPLE ENCOUNTER

LEARN FROM OTHERS'
MISTAKES

You only know what you want, when you know with clarity what you don't want. The main reasons people give up on their goals too quickly is because of the following:

Reason No 1: Environment

Their Environment is not empowering enough to support their growth. I don't care how positive you are, if you are around people who continue to bring you down and focus on the negative aspects, then you too will focus on the negatives and give up on following through. One of the main reasons I became very successful at a young age, was because the majority of my clients were very successful entrepreneurs and they enabled me to keep driving myself forward regardless of my setbacks.

Quick Action Exercise:

Decide to be around people who are "ahead in the game" than you. Do this at least 2 - 3 times a month. This might be going to events, going to networking meetings or inviting people to meet up for a coffee so you can pick their brains.

Reason No 2: Poor Education

Traditional education primes most people to work for someone else for the rest of their lives. The importance of upgrading your skill set is vital today. Remember that you get paid for the value you can deliver in an hour, not per hour that you work. The more skills that you take on board and the more you grow and learn, the more you earn. It really is that simple.

Elon Musk is one of the most successful entrepreneurs in the world and he continues to be an avid reader and learner because he knows that in order to keep pushing the boundaries, he must be ahead in the game for the most advanced ideas.

Quick Action Exercise:

Decide to upgrade your learning and plan your day to fit in at least 60 mins of extra learning to support you on your journey.

Reason No 3: Poor Mindset

Our mental training will either empower or disempower us and it's up to us to realise how often we spend time in positive emotion vs negative emotion. The fact of the matter is, if you consistently spend time in more positive emotion, you will achieve a lot more. If you consistently spent time in negative emotion you will get a lot less done.

Emotional Management is our ability to understand our emotions, where they come from, what the signal under the emotion is telling us, why we procrastinate, why we get overwhelmed and how to avoid these emotions on a daily basis.

Once you've managed and mastered the ability to train your brain, you can achieve anything that you set your mind to. Anything is possible. I know that may sound like a bold statement however, if you're willing to put the work in, you can quickly change your focus from the negative to the positive and ensure a positive outcome. That's why it's imperative you have a powerful environment to support the changes you make. Many people don't realise that their mindset is constantly working against them, making it harder to achieve their goals.

Quick Action Exercise:

Score yourself on the following barometer

Abundance thinking   vs   Scarcity thinking

10 9 8 7 6 5 4 3 2 1 0 1 2 3 4 5 7 8 9 10

If you truly come from a place of abundant thinking, you realise that there is enough for everyone to win together. You don't live in fear of money because you know that your skills can earn any amount of money that you truly want. You share business contacts, deals, commission with those around you, because again you know that there is an evergreen amount of money available to all of you. Mastering your finances is made possible today if you're willing to invest in yourself. Your most valuable asset is your mind. The more you invest in your mind, the richer you will become.

Reason No 4: Lack Of Accountability

The truth is, unless you tell someone your goals or have someone hold you accountable to your actions, you will not follow through with your plans. The brain is always looking for a way out, the path of least resistance and this is easy when nobody is holding you accountable and providing constructive feedback.

The one asset that we all have the same of and don't ever get back is our time. When you are accountable to the right person, you will surprise yourself at how much more you get done in a 24-hour period. I credit those who held me accountable for my actions for my success and the resilient mindset that I have today.

Quick Action Exercise:

Get a mentor or join an online accountability program. There are many to choose from and I too have many options for you. Most of all, it has to be right for you so that you get the results that you want.

Reason No 5: Lack Of The Right Mentor

I'm sure you have heard of the phrase, 'Monkey see, monkey do?' Learning by observing others is the quickest and most effective way to learn, it's the reason why apprenticeships are so valuable. In business, you can climb the ladder quickly by learning from someone who is ahead of you.

It's how we all learn valuable life skills. You didn't just wake up one day and decide that you could tie your shoe laces, right? You were taught by someone who had already learnt the shoe tying process and had the skills to teach you.

The same is true for everything you want in your life. It can all be achieved with the right guidance and support. You may wonder how or where on earth to find a mentor and to look out for, to ensure that it's the right option for you.

This is what I suggest:

Pay someone who has the results you want

Pay someone that can teach you effectively

Pay someone that is happy daily

If they fit the criteria above, I would suggest going ahead and investing into a mentor to help speed up your learning curve. I have invested into hundreds of mentors and their programs. I have learnt from some of the best and I have spent over £500,000 on my education alone to get me where I am today.

THE 7 KEY ELEMENTS OF WEALTH ™ is one of my great mentoring programs that covers everything you really need to start seeing incredible results in the most important seven key areas in your life. Most programs fail to cover the depth that is required for people to truly be successful today. Which is why I have included so much content for you to refer to.

You need to get these seven essential elements under control if you want to do the things that you want to do, live life on your terms and reach a higher level of happiness and fulfilment.

The problem today is that although people know the importance of these areas, they get overwhelmed and then don't follow through, they don't have any systems in place to truly get a full understanding of how to get the life they deserve.

If you haven't already done so, score yourself on the **THE 7 KEY ELEMENTS OF WEALTH** ™ so that you have a benchmark of where you are right now, so you know what you need to aim for. Clarity of where you are starting from right now is vital.

There is no need to exaggerate your scores. Most people overestimate their scores to say they are better than they actually are, however if you do that, you are only misleading yourself. Nobody but you cares about your scores, so be real and honest with yourself.

If you go to the bank and ask to borrow money, there is no point in lying to the bank saying the business can pay a greater amount of money back than it can, because when the business can't pay, the bank will come for you. Most people take a while to be honest with themselves, to be able to say you're not quite where you want to be is a very important self discovery process.

CHAPTER 17

THE 7 ELEMENTS OF WEALTH

CHANGE YOUR FOCUS,
CHANGE YOUR LIFE

THE 7 ELEMENTS OF WEALTH

LEGACY

WORK MISSION

MONEY

TIME

RELATIONSHIP

EMOTIONAL MANAGEMENT

HEALTH

You'll have noticed that I've referred to **THE 7 KEY ELEMENTS OF WEALTH** ™ many times throughout the book and that is because it is absolutely crucial to your success. These are seven fundamental areas that you need to address in order to create the life and achieve the level of success that you deserve.

Element 1: Health

Give yourself a score on your current health 1-10. Make sure you are as honest as possible with yourself, don't be too harsh or too generous. It's not rocket science, if you have poor levels of health it's very difficult to be productive, be in a good emotional state. Being healthy is what true wealth is all about. You can't consider yourself to be wealthy if you have poor health, no energy or capacity to be vibrant in your day. Most people only appreciate their health when they are at risk of losing it. If you are currently in poor health and are able to change it, I encourage you to look past your current challenges and embrace making changes to get healthier. The healthier you are, the more vibrant, energetic and successful you'll be.

Quick Action Exercise:

Rate yourself 1-10

Element 2: Emotional Management

Give yourself a score on your Emotional Management 1-10 of how fulfilled you are in this key area of your life. Your emotional management is your ability to manage your daily emotional state, especially when you are under pressure and things are not going your way. How often do you spend time in negative energy versus positive energy? Do you find yourself stuck in overwhelm or procrastination? What is your preferred learning style - visual, auditory, kinesthetic or logical? How well do you know yourself, what's important to you and what do you want to achieve? Does your ego look silly or weak stop you from learning new skills and taking yourself out of your comfort zone? Does your ego tell you that you don't need to learn anymore, as you already know it all? How easily do you interact with those challenging relationships? How do you react to fear and do you overcome rejection easily? Can you take on feedback without taking it personally?

Quick Action Exercise:

Rate yourself 1-10

Element 3: Relationships

Give yourself a score on your current relationships 1-10 of how fulfilled you are in this key area. Look at the relationships in your life and recognise that it is probably the area that will give you the most pain and pleasure in life. Even if you are someone who's not interested in relationships, I want you to know all business today is built around relationships. The stronger the relationship, the better the business will be. If you want to be successful in any area of your life, mastering your relationships is key. Think about how easily you interact and manage those unavoidable yet challenging relationships?

There are three areas that you'll need to consider namely; the relationship with yourself, the relationship with others and the relationship with your intimate partner. Give yourself 3 separate scores in these areas.

Quick Action Exercise:

Rate yourself 1-10

3.1: Self 1-10

3.2: Others 1-10

3.3: Intermate 1-10

Element 4: Time

Give yourself a score on your quantity of time 1-10 of how fulfilled you are in this key area. If you have no time in your life, then your score will be nearer to 0. If you have true ownership of your time, then your score will be nearer 10. A high score in this area is what you want to achieve as it allows you to go anywhere and work anywhere in the world. You may want to develop or already have a skill set that is easily transferable or maybe you aim to have a business that you can walk away from that still takes care of itself when you are not there? When you have complete ownership over your business, you can spend time doing what you want, where you want and with whom you want. You can even come and spend a month in Bali with me at the end of the year.

Quick Action Exercise:

Rate yourself 1-10

Element 5: Career/Work/Mission

Give yourself a score on level of happiness attached to these key areas of your life 1-10. How fulfilled are you in this key area in general? What can you do to ensure that you are achieving as much as you possibly can each day? I tend to find that the higher the score, the happier you are. People who have a higher level of skill and who invest in themselves tend to be happier because they can link ambition and progression in their roles to fulfilment. Generally those who are at the lower end of the score in this key area, tend to feel stuck in a rut and don't embrace training or development easily for one reason or another. The important thing to remember is that no matter where you are right now, you can make a change for the better.

Quick Action Exercise:

Rate yourself 1-10

Element 6: Finances

Give yourself a score attached to your Finances 1-10 of how fulfilled do you feel in this key area of your life? You may want a little more or possibly even a lot more so that you can do all the things that make you happy and give you a sense of purpose. Whilst money isn't everything, it is a means to enable you to do good and make a change in the world. Generally speaking, if we earn more money and do good things with it, we will increase our score in this area. Find a way to serve others, provide value whilst doing something you love and you'll find that abundant wealth is simply a by-product. If all you aim to achieve is more money, then you'll always be chasing it but never get it.

With my online program I take people through the 6 key levels of money:

Level 1: Hand to mouth

Level 2: End of the month

Level 3: Financial freedom

Level 4: Scaling

Level 5: Impact

Level 6: Philanthropy

Quick Action Exercise:

Rate yourself 1-10 & which level of money are you at now and where do you want to progress to?

Element 7: Legacy

Give yourself a score on your Legacy 1-10 of how fulfilled you are in this key area of your life. Legacy is what you stand for, what difference you are making in the world. What do people say behind your back when you leave the room? What kind of person are you? Do you have any charities that you support? Do you spend time weekly, monthly giving back beyond yourself to a great cause?

Once a year I take a very special group of people on my Master Leadership Program to Bali. The program is very intense and on one of the days, I take people to see a school for disadvantaged children that we support. They get a chance to play with the children, take stock of their lives and appreciate how privileged they are. This is one of three charities that I support. The importance of supporting those who are less fortunate than ourselves, enables us all to create a real difference in the world, to count our blessings every day. When people witness how happy the children are, how simplistic their lives are compared to most children in the Western world, the impact and experience is humbling and life changing on so many levels.

Quick Action Exercise:

Rate yourself 1-10 on your legacy.

Now that you have assessed yourself in all seven key elements, you can focus on areas you need or want to improve on first, as a priority. Start with areas that will influence and impact the other areas of your life significantly.

Simply pick 2 key areas now that are the most important to you.

I appreciate that they are all important to you, however to avoid mass overwhelm, I suggest taking two areas first that you can focus on. This will enable you to stay more upbeat and in tune with yourself. The key is to improve your scores massively. The higher the scores across these 7 Elements of Wealth, the happier and more fulfilled you will be.

A major problem today is feeling or becoming overwhelmed. Whilst their intentions are good, most people want to focus on all the things they need to do at the same time. The problem with this is that it leads to overwhelm and this very quickly links to feelings of being stuck, lost and depressed.

When you are overwhelmed, you can do one of two things namely; chunking up or chunking down. Let me explain what I mean.

I have suggested that you choose two areas to focus on to start with. This may be too much for you right now. You may find that choosing one area to focus on is all you can handle. That's absolutely fine, start with what is most important to you and focus solely on that. This is chunking down.

If on the other hand you choose an area you want to work on and then find that you are becoming too specific and focusing on details right down the track, you need to step back and look at the bigger picture. This is called chunking up.

Just as taking on too many areas at the same time can stifle your progress, getting lost in details can have the same effect. You will know which camp you are more likely to naturally fall into, so adapt your approach accordingly.

It is difficult to say which element to start with. Only you know which would serve you the most and where you'd get results quickest. In general, most people tend to pick Element 4, Element 5, Element 6 to get sorted first, which is what I did.

Element No 4 - Time which includes time management, time for self, freeing up time by systemising the business.

Element No 5 - Work Career finding something you love doing more than what you currently are, to give you a better quality of life.

Element No 6 – Finances allowing you more freedom to make better choices.

These are important and if you start with these then it becomes easier to work on the others as you have more time, focus and money.

The problem is that you also need:

Element No 1 - Health to be effective and productive.

Element No 2 - Emotional Management to stay motivated and manage your inner voice or critic.

Element No 3 - Relationships help you in all areas of personal and business life.

So the key is to improve them one at a time. You will get them all sorted over a period of time so start where you can, master that and move onto the next. Over the years, thousands of students found that once they'd mastered these key areas, their lives were unrecognisable and they felt more fulfilled and happy than they ever thought possible. This can and will be true for you if you trust the process and master each individual element.

CHAPTER 18

MASTER HABITS
FOR A LIFETIME THAT
EMPOWER YOU

There is a range of information available today about how you make or break habits. All of them point to a set period of time that allow new behaviours and habits to develop and become hardwired, second nature even, without any conscious effort on your part. As we go through this next chapter, you will recognise and understand the patterns of habit development more clearly. This is helpful when you are finding it tough to stick at something new and unfamiliar, as you'll understand that it is just part of the process. It will help you trust the process and master successful habits.

The 4 key stages of developing successful habits

When we are learning something for the first time, in order for it to become a habit, it has to go through 4 key stages of development, until it is hardwired and happens automatically, without effort.

Do you remember:

Stage 1: Unconscious Incompetence

Stage 2: Conscious Incompetence

Stage 3: Conscious Competence

Stage 4: Unconscious Competence

The important thing to remember is that repetition is key. Your success and results depend on the number of times you attempted to create the habit each day. The more you practise a behaviour, the easier it becomes to master. Did you know that you can make or break a new habit within 49 days? With this in mind and to help you get results, I put together a video module and audio series that is delivered daily over 49 days to help support you to massively improve your scores in these key areas with step by step processes. You can find out more about that at the end of the book.

8 simple steps to help you create and break habits

1. Keep it simple

Most people over complicate what it is they want to change. The more simplistic you keep the behaviour you want to change, the easier it becomes. Rather than thinking about all the behaviours that you want to change, simply start with the most important behaviour first. Once you've changed the first you can move on to the next one. Focusing on one behaviour at a time is an important skill to master and you'll get better results quicker.

2. Daily Focus

Commit to practicing the new behaviour you want to engrain as often as possible everyday, without fail. Most people get too distracted, take on too much and as a result, they get overwhelmed and end up either giving up or not mastering the new behaviour as they had intended. As you continue to focus on your daily routine, it will become second nature, hardwired and within a short period of time, you'll do it easily without even having to think about it.

3. Reinforce Good Behaviour

Remind yourself how well you did by creating your new behaviour at the end of each day. The more you reward and reinforce the big and small wins each day, the more likely it will become a part of you are. No matter what level you are at, who you are, I believe that we all need encouragement for taking the steps. Whilst it may sound silly and childlike, a simple pat on your back when you consistently do something well, is a powerful reinforcer and reminder of your effort. I actually pat myself on the back of my head, so my brain realises that in fact something successful has been achieved and my nervous system gets used to feeling good from accomplishing a task. It's a great feeling and I challenge you to have a go and test it for yourself.

4. Create A New Trigger Association

A trigger association is incredibly powerful and using one is so effective, definitely one of the best ways to unconsciously reprogram your mind to want to master the new behaviour. Every time you are doing the new behaviour, make sure that you are conscious of the words you are saying and of the sounds you are listening to. If you start to say, "I learn easily and effortlessly when learning new skills" when you first start learning a skill and you practise saying it out loud, you will find it easier. The more you tell yourself this, the easier it will be. This is what an associated trigger is and it can be verbal or physical. The more awareness you increase around your behaviours when doing something unfamiliar and new, the more aware you will be about the language you use and how this influences and impacts the experience you have.

5. Remove Visual Temptation

Be laser focused when you are learning a new habit as it is easy to be swayed and distracted by normal day to day things. Your visual input is very important and will aid or hamper your progress. Dr Milton Ericsson stated that every behaviour starts with a visual input. For instance, if you want to stop eating chocolate, you could remove all the chocolate from your house so you never see it. Over time you will begin to forget about it all together and the temptation will subside.

Similarly, you can use visual input to create focus of what you are working towards. You could create a vision board and position it where you see it repeatedly during the day, or pop post it notes on your wall to remind you of your schedule. You may even have a visual reminder on your phone of something that stimulates a positive association and empowers you to take action. Think how many times you see your phone during the day and how positive or inspired you'd feel if you had a visual trigger to motivate you. It's a waste of good inspirational space if you're not using that space wisely.

6. Practice feeling successful every day

When you know which new behaviour you want to achieve, you need to practice feeling what it would feel like once you have mastered it. For instance, if you want to go to the gym, you can imagine yourself at the gym, feeling proud that you got up early and that you are taking charge of your health. Take time each day to feel how great you'd feel once you have learnt this new behaviour. The clearer you are about how good it will feel or be for you, the more likely you are to make sure that it happens.

7. Practice feeling the disappointment of not being successful

Whilst I don't want you to dwell in a negative headspace, it is really helpful to notice the disappointment you'd feel if you weren't strong enough to master the new behaviour that you have chosen. Using the gym example above, you could focus on how you currently feel about your body, how that impacts on all the other areas of your life and how you'll have the same challenges (possibly even worse) until you change your behaviour. This is a great motivator to get you out of bed and into the gym.

8. The gift of time

Have you heard the saying, 'The trees that grow the slowest produce the best fruit, fences that are put up quickly fall down fast.' Taking time to think about your behaviours will steer your future in the long term, is well worth doing. A small change to your daily routine, will over time, give you incredible results. Think about what your life will be like if you got up just 20 minutes earlier and spent time planning your day, reminding yourself of you life purpose or even doing your morning mantra. It's so interesting, most people will overestimate what they can do it one year and then underestimate what they can co in 10 years. Start thinking about the long term goals and focus on implementing small improvements each day that bring you one step closer towards your goal. By doing this you'll find yourself a lot healthier, wealthier and happy because of it.

CHAPTER 19

CHANGE YOUR
PAST PERCEPTIONS
AND MEMORIES

CHANGE YOUR FUTURE

Cognitive retraining is a much deeper process than just visualisation but is really effective at helping you develop successful habits. Ideally, I'd recommend that you do it with a trained coach before applying it on yourself. You will get much better results doing it with someone else who is objective and emotionally detached from the behaviours you need or want to change. We all find it difficult to pinpoint our blind spots and we don't often recognise that we behave or react in a certain way until it is pointed out to us. Having a supportive, skilled professional to highlight weaknesses and areas you can improve in will only stand you in good stead and you'll become happier and more successful because of it.

Viewing a problem from a different perspective or a fresh point of view is a lot more helpful than approaching it in the same way and never resolving it. It is why you ask for a second opinion when you don't get the outcome you wanted.

Not only do you get an objective point of view but it's a lot quicker to get a coach on board to help you identify and resolve your weak spots. Again, this is only to build you up and enable you to move forward quickly and excel at everything you want to achieve. Imagine how much stronger you'd be if you knew your weaknesses and took steps to improve them? Overtime you would feel physically and emotionally invincible.

When I was younger, I created a range of unwanted behaviours that slowly and surely started to disempower me daily. What I noticed was that like all behaviours, the more I practised them, the better I became at executing them. This is true for everyone and all behaviours that we choose to keep alive and practice persistently.

If you're scared and fearful of certain situations, you'll find that they get even bigger in your mind and have a stronger effect on your life over time. It might not seem like a life changing fear to begin with, but the more you practice it, the more areas of your life, as well as those around you, it will impact.

As a child, I believed that I would get car sick. This belief was created unintentionally and later massively impacted my entire family's life. The behaviour was set up when I was being driven back from school one day and I was reading a book in the back of the car. The combination of looking down at the book and being in the car made me feel sick. It wasn't long before I was sick in the car. My brain coded that experience as "I can't drive in the car without being sick." The belief that I would always be sick when driving, quickly filtered into other modes of transport including trains, boats and planes. This meant that family holidays were affected as my parents simply couldn't physically take me anywhere without me being sick all over the place. Once I recognised the original trigger and that it was for all these events, I was able to change my reactions and I haven't been ill in a car, plane, train or boat for over 14 years.

Now you might not think that is a big deal. What happens in your brain when you change the trigger association is very empowering. Your brain starts to think, if this is no longer a problem like it used to be, then what else am I capable of achieving? The brain starts thinking that anything else is possible and steers you in the direction of self belief and achievement.

I'm going to take you through a very effective and powerful cognitive **Trigger Change Pattern™** training process. Please imagine that we're going through this together now and you will get much better results. You could also do this with someone who you trust if it is more helpful to have someone do it in person with you.

A lot of positive psychology cognitive retraining techniques were developed from the study of very unwell people and their ability to get better by using these processes. Instead of focusing on traditional medicine, the study focused on how people became unwell in the first place. They discovered tools and techniques that people did in their mind to allow a new path to occur. This was the complete opposite to what they had expected and the results were phenomenal.

The **Trigger Change Pattern** ™ For Unwanted Behaviours:

Step 1: Identify the behavioural pattern you want to change

Close your eyes and think of the pattern you want to change.

Step 2: Recall the earliest memory of this behavioural pattern

Keep it simple and see if you can remember the first memory of how the behavioural pattern began. Maybe you get nervous before you are meant to speak in front of an audience? Maybe when someone looks at you in a certain way you feel uncomfortable? Maybe when your partner says something or looks at you in a certain way it sets off a defensive or disempowering feeling? Maybe you find yourself distracted easily and wanting to do anything other than what you're supposed to, knowing full well that you need to do the first task? Maybe you go to eat something just because you see it and don't even remember going through a choice to decide to eat it first?

Step 3: Visualise earliest memory of the initial trigger

Once you have the earliest memory of the initial trigger, create a picture from that memory. See yourself in the memory so that you have a visual input. Now go moments before the memory was created, before the trigger was set, now, hold that picture in your mind, just for a moment and then I want you to make the picture in your mind, black and white. Notice that as you do that, you feel less emotion towards that memory, towards the picture. You should have less and less emotion towards the picture. I want you to push the picture, the memory as far away from you as possible until the picture is small, dark and grey and you can barely see the picture. This will be your old picture.

Step 4: Create a new picture

In this picture this is how you can see and feel how you ideally would like to when the trigger is set off again. This will be your new empowered behaviour. Imagine that the trigger is set off, and you feel the way you want to instead.

Maybe in the past you got nervous before you were meant to speak in front of an audience and now you see yourself confidently standing on stage, speaking with ease, speaking loudly and the audience are loving your speech as they clap furiously at your sparkling charisma?

Maybe in the past when someone looked at you in a certain way instead of feeling nervous you now feel confident and like it was meant to be and you enjoy them appreciating you?

Maybe in the past your partner said something or looked at you in a certain way instead of setting off a disempowering feeling, it now triggers an overwhelming sense of love for your partner?

Maybe in the past when it was time for you to do a task instead of finding yourself distracted you can now see yourself motivated and excited about doing it at speed and feeling really good because you have achieved what you wanted to achieve?

Maybe in the past when you wanted to eat something instead of eating it all and feeling guilty, you see yourself pushing the plate away, pushing the food away and feeling really healthier for not eating it?

Now you have this new empowered picture. I want you to make it as bright and colourful as possible. Notice the more colours in the picture, the more appealing it becomes for you. Create more sound in the picture and as you do, notice that it allows you to enjoy the experience more. Notice as you do that, you are more aware of the positive feelings that you feel in and around your core, either in your stomach, or in your heart or all around your body in some shape or form. As you notice these great feelings, notice how your breathing changes and adapts, maybe it gets deeper and stronger. Notice your thoughts in your head. Allow yourself to say things that support and empower you to move forward and progress rather than regress. Stand the way you are meant to stand and notice that when your shoulders are pulled back and your chest is out, that you feel stronger in who you are and what you are about.

Step 5: Move your new picture to the lower left hand corner in your mind

Move the picture on the lower left hand of the screen in your mind. Just like you would minimise a computer screen window on a laptop or a desktop computer. Keep the new picture burning bright in the left hand corner and go back to your old picture for a second. Access the old picture and bring it in front of your mind. Notice you feel nothing as its dark and grey.

Step 6: Reduce the old picture and replace with your new picture

We are going to swap the new picture over the old picture and blow out the old picture and all it means to you. We are going to do this as quickly as I say the words. Go and click your fingers at the same time. The faster you do this the better it is.

Do this as quickly as possible

1, 2, 3 - GOOOOOO - (Click your fingers at the same time)

Open your eyes then close your eyes straight away.

Step 7: Rinse and repeat above steps

Then repeat the steps until the old picture is no longer there.

Now if you followed the steps, what you will notice is that if you get the trigger change on the earliest memory of when the behaviour was first created, then you will change the initial association. The more you practise this as a technique, what you'll notice is you no longer remember or notice the disempowered feeling any more.

You may find it difficult accessing your older memories. This is very common, just take more time to practise it and it will become easier. You can use this in any area of your life to rapidly change unwanted behaviours. I'd suggest that you consider the seven elements of wealth and eliminate restricting and limiting beliefs around those areas.

It is truly life changing and the ripple effect is pretty astounding. Here are some case studies I'd like to share to inspire you to think more about what you'd like to change in different areas of your life.

Business

One of my clients had a fear of heights and we changed his fear using this technique. After getting over his fear of heights, he found the courage to make other changes in his life. Starting his own business and standing up for himself at work to enable him to get a pay rise.

Love

Another client used this technique for getting over an old partner who she'd split up with and hadn't moved on in 10 years. She was miserable and stuck. After she changed the association, she tripled the profit margins in her business and found a new partner who was more in tune with her vision and values.

Money

I had a client that used this around association with money, specifically feeling guilty for charging for her services. The results, she charged the true value for her service and she got better results from her clients, as they felt happier too. Her reputation grew quickly and she increased the number of her clients coming to see her by 30 %.

Whatever you want to change, you can and you can improve your life in ways you never imagined. The more you practise it, the more you increase your awareness around your behaviours and you'll realise that you are in total control of your reality and behaviours that you thought were unconscious to you.

You are in control. Increase your ability to stay present, in the moment right now. Stop and take a moment to appreciate whatever you are experiencing in that moment and your life will be fuller.

CHAPTER 20

RESOLVE RELATIONSHIP
RESISTANCE AND RISE

LOVE THE PEOPLE IN YOUR
LIFE … NO MATTER WHAT

One of your biggest challenges as you become more successful is dealing with other people, respecting their beliefs, handling their opinions on what course of action you should take to achieve more in your life. As you continue to grow, you will begin to outgrow your partner, your friends and your family unless they also embrace change and growth. This is natural but can also be painful and will cause you lots of challenges. You need to be properly prepared to manage this.

Whilst you will be on a different journey to those around you, I would suggest that you continue to support your friends, partner and loved ones. This creates a new positive sense of identity of self for you and they are less likely to feel resentful or like they have 'lost' you.

Be sensitive and aware of your growth as it can be intimidating to those in your life. If they feel that you've outgrown them, they will want to hold you back and this creates unnecessary problems on your new path. As you are on a steep learning curve, you want to avoid constant friction in the way you conduct yourself.

It is good and important to have people in your life who think differently to you. For many people, most of the people who will most likely feel challenged with the new you, are those closest to you like your family.

Become a better communicator, a stronger leader and do not allow their doubt or negativity to bring you down. Show them by example how much better life can be and prove to them the results that you have in your life is purely because of your new actions and thought processes. Remember that everything you have become is all learnt and be confident that if you can do it, they can too. This is empowering and inspiring for those around you.

Let your results speak for themselves, don't ram your beliefs down their throats no matter how passionate you feel and how much you want to help them. Keep your opinions, your thoughts and your words of wisdom for those who are interested and want to know more. This will allow them to see things from your point of view when they are ready for it.

There are a range of different tools that enable people to understand belief structures on a much deeper level. Your continued growth and investment into your personal development will give you the ability to handle other people effectively at an advanced level.

Here are 4 of the advanced beliefs that will remarkably change your ability to interact with others.

1. Focus on understanding & listening to their point of view to reduce conflict

As soon as you actively listen to someone rather than trying to cut them off or talk over them, they'll be more open to listening to you in return. If someone says something to you, whether or not you agree with them you'll automatically create a deeper bond with one another. When you recognise that it is just their point of view, you'll be less defensive and more open to discussing their point of view and possibly even get them to see yours.

Example: Possible attack: "I think you should spend less time working on yourself and more time with the family."

Answer: I appreciate why you think that would be the right thing to do from your point of view. I respect why you think that is important for me to spend time with the family and that's why I'm spending time working on myself, so when I am with the family, I can give more of myself to the family and serve the family at a higher level."

Quick Action Exercise:

Think of a relationship in your life that needs healing. Consider seeing the situation from their point of view so that you could begin to forgive. At the end of your life would you regret not healing that relationship? At the end of your life if you didn't say the things you wanted to say to them, would you regret it? If the answer is yes to any of them, it's time to start going on a healing journey with that person. It seems easier and less painful to kick people out because they think differently until you have the skills to heal. Surely you'd prefer a healthy relationship instead of a void that the lack of it creates? As you become more successful it's vital that you develop the skills to manage and adapt to other people's behaviours more effectively to manage and avoid unnecessary conflict.

2. Respect their model of thinking to build a connection

We all have different ideas, perceptions and models of the world. We have different backgrounds, different experiences and different levels of education. These differences don't make anyone's perspective more or less valuable or relevant than anyone else's. As soon as you can respect others' differences, you can find an effective line of communication and create a deeper bond of finding resolution if there is friction. You will gain an unconscious agreement with someone as soon as you can convey a respect for their thinking, so this is a vital skill to master.

It's not always easy and often it can be painful especially if the person in question is somebody really close to you. For many years I thought badly of my father because I didn't respect his level of thinking. He has always told me to stick to what was safe, and once I understood why he had told me that repeatedly, we were able to move a step closer to healing our relationship. I learnt that he was driven to protect me because he had been burned when he started his own business. What he was really trying to communicate was I could avoid making the same mistakes that he had.

Underneath all behaviour, there is a driver for good. Sometimes it's hard to find, sometimes it can be misguided however, under the layer of negative emotion there is a signal that we can take a powerful lesson from, to enable us a massive amount of growth.

Quick Action Exercise:

Think of people that you have had conflict with before. Can you practise seeing the conflict that you had from a different point of view? A point of view that would allow you to think and feel differently about the situation and allow you to move further forward?

3. Change the behaviour, change the experience

Recognise that people are not their behaviours, they are just people with certain behavioural traits. When you look past the behaviour, you can accept the person and work on changing their behaviour in the moment.

This belief enables you to let go of any judgment and to realise that people are forever changing their behaviours according to the context they are surrounded by. If you can consider that people are not their behaviours, you'll begin to see behaviours as ever changing.

For example there were times in your life you were angry. Anger is a behaviour that you displayed at a particular point in relation to a certain stimulus. There were times in your life that you were happy, and there were times that you were sad. No matter what emotion or behaviour you displayed you weren't that behaviour all the time.

People change from moment to moment and portray different behaviours according to the situation. Those who train good behaviours over a time, spend a majority of time adopting the characteristics of these behaviours. Those who train disempowering behaviours, also train these for a period of time.

Begin to realise that people can change their behaviours with practise and volition. They can set an intent to be a better version of themselves by taking action and free themselves from limiting beliefs and associated patterns of behaviour. Once this belief and understanding of others is engrained, you will find yourself living with a deeper level of happiness and compassion for other people. You'll automatically judge less and allow yourself to be happier as an individual regardless of negativity in your life and this just gets better and better overtime.

Quick Action Exercise:

Have you ever noticed yourself arguing with a partner and right in the middle, your phone rang? Think about how quickly you adopted a new polite behaviour to speak to that person on the phone? It's pretty instant right?

Have you ever noticed that you made someone laugh in the moment that they were super angry at you and for whatever reason they could no longer remain angry with you with the same level of intensity? This is a perfect example of what we have just covered.

Notice the next time that you are angry, sad, frustrated, lonely. Go outside and practise the **MANTRA** exercise with intensity and notice how you feel afterwards. Notice if it changed your emotional state and how you felt about yourself compared to how you felt when you first walked outside. This is powerful stuff. It's free, healthy and organic so use it as much as you can to change your state or the state of others for better outcomes.

4. Realise that people are doing the best they can with the resources they have

This new belief allows forgiveness to occur in your life when you consider that every moment, every person is doing the best they can with the resources they have. If you can adopt the thinking that, up to this point in time that person has acquired their current experience, knowledge, their decision making, capabilities to help them deal with the situation as best they can.

Maybe they've not had the experience of reading this book like you, maybe they've not had the experiences that you have, maybe they're not as open minded as you are and because you have taken up these new skills, you will be far more skilled to deal with others. Allow yourself to forgive people for doing the best they can in that moment, even if it didn't serve you, notice that they were doing the best that they could. When people make mistakes and are forgiven, they usually take heed, learn from it and don't allow it to happen again. This serves both parties and more importantly, you can feel good about allowing forgiveness to take place.

When you can adopt this as a belief you will enable yourself to forgive quicker. For example, I now respect my dad's way of thinking and model of the world with regards to his suggestion that I should just stick to what I know. I can tell you with certainty that that was not the case when I was younger and had I known what I'm teaching you now, things would have been very different.

As a young gym cleaner, he would say to me "Edward, stick to what you know." I didn't know much as a young boy so the problem with that way of thinking meant I wouldn't learn anything new. My day grew up in a different era where job security was crucial.

Overtime I understood and began to see why his thinking was the way it was. He was doing the best he could with the resources and the information that he had. He is still today, unaware of the potential of starting up your own business, the power of social media, the power of online marketing etc. I respect his point of view and know he was always acting from a position of care and love towards me even at times when it didn't feel like it. His inability to communicate and demonstrate it effectively caused unnecessary friction and that has been resolved. We both respect each others' intentions that they come from a place of love.

Quick Action Exercise:

If you were to forgive someone in your life, who would it be? I appreciate that maybe it may be too hard for you to allow this to happen so early on in our relationship however, if you were to forgive someone who would it be? If I were to forgive someone it would be ... Remember the longer you hold onto a negative emotion, the more it grows inside, the more it affects other behaviours. Once you allow yourself the gift of forgiveness, there is a whole load of possibilities that can be opened up for you. Maybe it's time to forgive yourself?

When you have an argument, your brain waves rise. The higher they get, the more it affects your behaviour. As soon as the brain goes up over 97 beats a minute, which is usually caused by anxiety, it becomes overwhelmed. The beta waves in the brain become more erratic and the effect of stress overwhelms the person.

Stress creates certain behavioural patterns. More often than not, you'll say things you don't mean and then repeat yourself over and over again almost as though your brain has got stuck on a loop you can't get out of.

Just take a moment and if you would stand up and get some new perspective with me.

I'm going to give you the 4 most powerful phrases in the world.

This is nothing new as you have definitely heard these words before. People use them without really thinking about meaning behind them. The key is to practise 100 % saying them when you are truly committed to the meaning and you are using them with complete integrity and commitment. Do not use them for personal gain in any way, shape or form or they lose the real impact of them.

These originally came from an ancient Hawaiian healing prayer, which has been used to practise the art of reconciliation and forgiveness. Dr. Ihaleakala Hew Len, has done the most research into this area and has published a range of different books around the healing practices that he carried out using this. Sceptics tried to debunk his work, saying they wanted more evidence and documented proof of the success of this process.

Rising to the challenge, he looked for a way to give the process more evidence and background. He applied for a position in a high security unit in Hawaii State Hospital where the criminally and mentally ill were kept. They had a huge turnover of staff because they feared for their safety. Being around convicted murderers and rapists on a daily basis was not fun or uplifting.

Dr Hew Len agreed to do the work. He had one condition. The people allowed him to work with the patients in his unique way. He never met face to face with them. Instead, as he opened and read their files, he repeated the same four phrases over and over again. Little by little, the patients started to get better and show visible signs of changing their behaviour towards one another.

What was happening is that he was going through and experiencing their problems. As he went through each of the patients' files, he looked within himself at whatever came up and what he needed to let go of. As he did the "cleaning process" on himself, with no direct patient contact, the patients improved.

The inmates and patients' physical shackles and restraints were removed and within the next few years, the entire ward of criminally and or mentally ill patients were considered cured and the ward was closed down.

Being curious by nature, I have used the same process with thousands of my clients and have achieved wonderful results. People have often come to me for business advice and have left cleaning their entire past out which in turn, has had a huge knock on effect for them being wonderfully happy and fulfilled.

Whilst I'm not suggesting that you are a criminal or mentally unwell, I believe we all pick up negative emotions and without being able to let go of these emotions, we get a new experience to life because of it. Most people will never move forward because they are always held back by these negative experiences, some of which they aren't even aware of.

Most people have experienced being let down by a parent in some way, shape or form. Being let down by a partner, having expected failure or rejection in their personal or professional life is unfortunate and hurtful. This cleaning process enables you to experience completely letting go of all the things that have held you back and igniting a spark for a brighter future.

In order to forgive others, you need to take 100 % responsibility for whatever you experience in your life. With this belief system, anything we see or feel comes from within, based on our past memories and the meaning we've given them.

Dr Hew Len says there is scientific evidence to show that we don't see people as they actually are, instead, we see our reactions to them. As we do more cleaning up, we are eradicating the memories from our unconscious mind that shows up as a problem. This process allows us to perceive the world through the eyes of our creator rather than through the warped eyes of our memories.

You must commit and repeat them over and over. Firstly, say them to yourself and a behaviour that you want to change. Notice how different you feel. Make sure you are in a safe space and you are comfortable, then take yourself through it.

Imagine different people in your life, good and bad relationships and clean those associations with those people. If possible add them into your **MANTRA ™** and allow them to be ingrained into who you are as a person. Repeat the following 4 phrases over and over again and notice what changes you feel inside.

I am sorry

Please forgive me

Thank you

I love you

If you say these 4 sentences over and over again, you will experience a huge sense of forgiveness to yourself and to others. Repeat them so often to yourself that they become hardwired in who you are and influence your day in many unexpected ways.

You can adapt and use these four sentences in any situation, personal and professional on a daily basis. I recently drove my car into the person in front of me. I wasn't paying enough attention whilst moving out of my car parking space. He was absolutely fuming and looked like he was about to blow a blood vessel. He came to my window, pounded on it and started shouting at me. He was in a complete state of rage.

I didn't have to even think about it. I said, "Oh my, I'm so sorry" and I truly meant it. 'Please forgive me I must've not been paying attention. Please allow me to pay for the damage, take my number and details and I will sort it out straight away." He replied, "Wow I didn't expect you to reply like that, I was getting ready for a fight." I said thank you for being so kind and not hitting me, I really appreciate that.

He was so shocked and taken aback. After inspecting the damage on his car, he replied "Do you know what, let's not worry about it, I will get a good friend of mine to sort it out, I'm sure it'll be fine."

Just before he got into his car I said, "I love the fact that you were able to accept my apology." He replied, "There's something special about you! You have a fantastic kind of energy about you." I again said, "Thank you for your kind reply. If you see it in me, it's in you too. Please take my number and if for any reason your friend can't sort out your car, I'm very happy to pay for it as it was my mistake. All the best and let me know."

If you embody these 4 powerful statements, no matter what has happened in the past or you believe to have happened, these 4 powerful statements can change your entire concept of them, if you are open and willing to test them.

People are like Cats or Dogs - Which one are you?

When dealing with other people, this is very useful to remember. It's quite normal to get very excited when learning new concepts and ideas. Applying them so that you become a better communicator is vital to your growth and development. You will find that when you speak to people you adapt how you communicate with them in order to create a bond or rapport. It can be helpful to think of your approach in terms of whether you are working with a cat or a dog.

Dog owners will tell you that when you feed them, you are the master and their dogs are ready and waiting for you to feed them. They'll do what you say, they're open to your commands and even find it fun and stimulating and above all, you are very important to them.

Cat owners will tell you that generally when you feed them, they're the master and will only eat when it suits them. They'll only do what you say when it suits them. They're not open to your suggestions and definitely ignore commands, unless it suits them. They couldn't care less about your point of view and they love the fact that you need them and not the other way around.

Neither is right nor wrong, better or worse. By recognising how best to communicate so you both get results, will save you a lot of time and effort.

Typically, cat personalities are not ready to hear what you are saying or what you have to offer yet. They're not open to new ways of thinking, they're not open to different beliefs yet. Most people spend their lives frustrated with others because they don't understand why that person can't see it from their perspective. The cat personality needs to take time to process the information how and when it suits them. There is absolutely nothing wrong with that, this is starting you on the journey to truly understanding that we're all very different.

When you spend more time with people who have more dog-like personalities, you'll find that they are easier to be around if you too are a dog personality. They are more open to new ideas and they are more open to different points of view. They are coachable, they listen, they're attentive, they want to do well with what you have given them.

Take a moment to consider yourself. Which one do you think you are? Are you open to new ideas, are you closed to other people? When someone you trust advises and gives you feedback, can you take it on board and progress because of it? Or do you need to question that feedback over and over again and then question your trust around that person?

Quick Action Exercise:

Think of people in your life who instantly stand out as having more dog like characteristics and think of others who have more cat like characteristics. Once you've done that, does it immediately highlight why you are having conflict with certain people? Can you change your behaviour around a cat in your life to manage them more effectively?

CHAPTER 21

BECOME THE ULTIMATE
VERSION OF YOURSELF

BE ACCOUNTABLE FOR ALL
YOUR ACTIONS

Many believe that the holy grail of life is to become enlightened, awakened and fulfilled. This only occurs when you commit to never ending improvement. Enlightenment, awakening and fulfilment is a state of complete understanding that you are in control of your own destiny and it is you who either creates or destroys your reality. You alone have achieved the current results in your life regardless of whether you consider them good or bad. The buddha classifies enlightenment as the lack of suffering.

People often ask me how I know if I'm fully enlightened and fully awake. My answer always is, "when you don't need to ask that question any more, when you have no suffering regardless of what life throws at you. If you commit to never ending self improvement and accept the universal law of growth, then you are well on the way."

By taking ownership over each of the seven elements of wealth, you'll take a step closer to becoming more fulfilled. It is easy to focus on one dimension of your life, forgetting that there are many aspects to consider. When you solely focus on generating wealth or securing the relationship of your dreams, it's easy to forget about your health.

The only way to truly become happy and fulfilled is to look at life with a complete view. No element is more important than the other and none of them can be overlooked. It's essential that each step of the journey is focused around mastering each element and then moving on to the next challenge that lies ahead. Growing your scores in each element awakens new challenges, new opportunities to become the very best version of yourself.

Commit to continued growth in all areas of your life. Everything in the universe either grows or dies. A flower is either growing or dying, a business is either growing, becoming more effective, streamlining staying more competitive or it's dying. A relationship is either growing deeper in love and trust for one another or else it's staying the same or getting worse, which leads to a breakdown or a parting of ways. Just because two partners are together, doesn't mean that their relationship is growing together.

Quick Action Exercise:

Quickly write down what level would you gauge yourself on never ending improvement

growth? How often are you investing into your learning, taking courses, focusing on expanding yourself, reading books, taking online courses, listening to podcasts, watching YouTube videos that stimulate your thought and knowledge?

Rate and score yourself 1-10.

Success is not a straight line

Many people expect to decide what they want, make some quick decisions, follow through by taking some action and want to see the results straight away. Taking this approach only leads to frustration and often, burn out. It is better to consider your new venture as though you were planting a seed.

When you plant a seed, you can't expect to see the fruit straight away. It takes a lot of time, nurturing and effort before you get any fruit. You need to plant it in the correct soil, water it, ensure that it has the right nutrition and is nurtured and protected through the different seasons.

Just like a seed, you too need to be watered, protected and nurtured through the seasons to continue on your journey to reach higher levels.

At the start of a flight, a plane will set its destination and course on the most efficient route. Then it'll spend the majority of the time adjusting its route depending on weather, according to wind speeds until it's back on course, on schedule and flying in the right direction.

Success is the same. Most people think it will look like this.

WHAT PEOPLE THINK SUCCESS WILL LOOK LIKE

ACTION  **SUCCESS**

WHAT IT ACTUALLY LOOKS LIKE

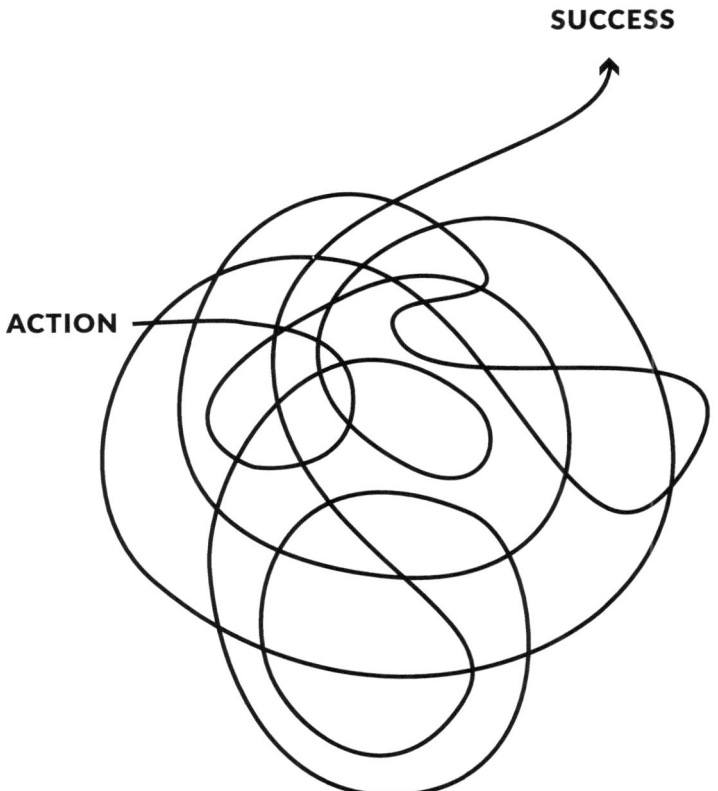

Your growth is constant, even when you can't see results provided you keep pushing yourself to move forward. The key is to accept that you will hit periods called a plateau when you stick at the same level for a period of time. When you don't have someone to hold you accountable or guide you at this stage, you'll more than likely regress back to the **CAVE ™**.

The cave is a place where people give up on their dreams. There are 4 essential things that happen in the **CAVE** ™. It is not a good place to be and best avoided where possible. By having someone hold you accountable, by having others around supporting you and making sure that you follow through on your actions, you can then avoid getting stuck in the **CAVE** ™.

On your journey towards success, you will discover that a lot of people stuck deep in their cave. When you are seeing results and enjoying the momentum of your efforts, it is important to not judge them because we all go through tough times. Once you are masterful at the skills you have learnt already, it becomes relatively easy to get people out of their cave and back playing in the game of life. Be aware of your own journey and realise if you're in fact stuck in the cave, don't stay long and get support if getting out is not as simple as you expected it to be.

How to avoid getting stuck in the **CAVE** ™

C - In the **Cave** ™ people **CONVINCE** themselves that the problem they're facing is completely immovable. They believe that there is nothing they can do about it. The problem becomes the reason they can't move forward and stunts their growth. They blame the problem and see it as the reason why they don't have the things they want in their lives.

A - In the **Cave** ™ people **ACCEPT** the problem as part of themselves rather than pushing against it. They blame others for their misfortune and to the existence of the problem in their life. In the cave it's easy to blame others for the problem than actually doing something about it.

V - In the **Cave** ™ people become **VERY** internally focused. Every day their primary focus is on themselves and why they feel so bad, rather than focusing on becoming stronger and helping others which would distract them and change their contrast frame.

E - **EVERYDAY** in the **Cave** ™ gets progressively worse and worse. The pain can either change someone and drive them out of the cave ™or they will slowly end up in a vicious destructive cycle.

The most important part of staying accountable is to make sure that you never give up on your dreams. You must get someone to keep you on track because you're only as good as the people that support you. You only have one life so make sure that you create a masterpiece. Make sure that when it comes to the end of your life, you have nothing to regret and you have done all the things you wanted to do. The most common things that people regret when they come to the end of their life is, not living their truth and doing the things that they truly want to do.

So, my friend, please go over the book a couple of times, share it with a friend so that you can both go through it together. My mission is that you spend your life living in your truth, connecting with your mission and making a dent in the universe. I want to say thank you for reading Money Mindfulness Daily. It has been a pleasure spending time with you. If I never see you again, I wish you all the best on your journey to success. If you want to take your journey to the next level with me, then it would be my pleasure to help you.

Quick Action Exercise:

Where are you going to be 6 months from now?

Where are you going to be 1 year from now?

Where are you going to be 3 years from now?

Where are you going to be 5 years from now?

MY JOURNEY
FROM ROCK BOTTOM
TO THE TOP OF
MY GAME

If it's ok, I'd like to share a bit of my background to show you that if I can change my life for the better, you can too. When people meet me, they quickly make assumptions about my journey, how easy everything happened for me and whilst this is far from the truth, it is a testament to how valuable the information you have in your hands, right now, is.

As I tell you about my journey, I want to reiterate that this is not to brag in any way, shape or form. I simply want to show you that I've honestly done my fair share of graft in business and mastering my mind. I'm confident that I'm fit to guide you to a better place and teach you the secrets to earning the life and money you deserve because of my experiences thus far.

I was recently running through a hotel reception on my way to the main ballroom where over 1,000 people were gathered in a room, cheering, lights flashing and music pumping. The atmosphere was electric, they were excited and waiting for me to arrive.

Moments before, I had been called up on stage. I paused to reflect and my mind said,

"... Seriously how the hell did this happen?..."

You may or may not know that I am currently an owner of a range of successful businesses, filling out events, making an impact and difference in the world.

My life has not always been this good. To be honest, it seemed like only yesterday that I was completely lost and hopeless...

It was a dark, cold November evening in 1993 when I stood on the edge of the railway platform, rain pouring down on me and soaking my clothes. I had given up on life and myself. There was nothing left. I remember feeling completely empty, sad and overwhelmed with negative thoughts. I had no purpose, no real meaning to my life and every day was a constant reminder to myself that, I just wasn't good enough. The tears streamed down my face as I awaited my fate.

If you'd been there with me, you would've been standing next to a very small, skinny boy, with acne all over his face, who had spent his life making people laugh and pretending everything was ok. However, inside he was lonely, confused and lost in the world.

I felt that I didn't really have the support I needed. At school I felt completely hopeless, usually at the bottom of the class in most classes and labelled as dyslexic from a young age, which was a stigma I really loathed. This meant I had linked a lot of pain to school and learning.

I felt useless in my home life as well. I had so many questions and couldn't get any answers. It seemed like I always got everything wrong. My relationship with my dad was slowly destroying me. For some reason, he seemed immensely irritated by me simply being in the world. We constantly clashed with one another. Nothing I did ever, no matter how hard I tried, seemed good enough for him.

Conversely my brother seemed to handle the storm in a very different way and my sister had a completely different experience. One evening after an altercation with my dad, he took out his frustration on me. At that moment, I chose to take a different path which lead me to the platform I was standing on ...

I could hear the train coming.

This would be my moment.

This would be my chance.

I felt a weird sense of bliss for a split-second, knowing that this would be the moment that the pain would stop.

I closed my eyes.

I leaned forward and awaited my fate to leave this world.

It's been said many times that there is a moment just before you die when you feel a sense of complete safety, complete peace and bliss. I believe I got a glimpse of all of that and more in that split second. It was something very pure and calm.

It's probably a bit like skydiving. Moments before you step out of the plane, your mind is full of fear. The moment you jump and begin to fall, your mind gets clarity and you can no longer contemplate what is happening around you and you give in to the sensation of letting go and just experiencing pure freedom. You become completely present and clear.

Back on the platform I suddenly felt two strong hands, heavy on my shoulders.

I was pulled back with force as the train whizzed past, narrowly missing my face.

I lay shocked on the floor, like a bug on its back, legs in the air, trying to catch my breath.

The man looked at me, equally stunned and horrified and asked if I was ok?

I let out a cry;

partly in shock,

partly in shame,

partly in guilt for what I had intended to do.

He helped me onto my feet and I gathered myself and the stuff I had with me.

He took me back home to make sure that I was ok.

I was back to what I wanted to escape from.

I still had no purpose, still had no meaning and I still didn't see the point of living.

I had battled with myself and my shortcomings for many years.

I had battled with my negative thoughts and limiting beliefs.

I had battled with my highly charged emotions.

I had constantly linked pain to school after failing so many times.

I had constantly linked pain to my home life after failing so many times there too.

However, after that moment in November everything seemed to change in some way or another. It was like I hit a threshold and my life had changed forever.

Everyday was different and if I'm honest, pretty tough. The difference in me was that I began to blame others less and I started a conscious journey of healing myself and my relationships with those closest to me. I tested out various methods of personal change and adopted those that worked.

Thankfully I was lucky to find good mentors and role models who were willing to help and support me. They enabled me to associate learning and growing with confidence and success, the complete opposite to my previous experience. I was able to go on a supported journey with them by my side. With that, I realised that I had a new mission and purpose in life. I decided to dedicate my life to serving others. It was time to pay the good that I had received forward and enable others to change their lives and do good too. I wanted to create a ripple effect and touch as many lives as possible.

Many of us go through hard times and I'm sure that you have faced some tough times too? I believe it's what we learn about ourselves, and how we deal with those times, that impact our future for the better. Dealing with adversity, is a powerful contributor to success and increasing your earning potential if you allow it to be.

Within a 3 year period, I had changed my life in so many ways that it was almost unrecognisable. My thinking was different, my outlook on life was more positive and this enabled me to create and find opportunities everywhere. My drive and determination were on a completely different level too.

I started my first business when I was 16, working for free as a coach and a personal trainer. That was a long time ago, when no one really knew about my service. I remember telling my dad, "I'm going to change people's lives and help people." He looked at me and paused, "Edward, you are 16 years old. You look about 10, and you haven't even lived yet. How are you ever going to help someone else change their life? You have not even lived yourself!" He had a valid point.

It wasn't easy by any stretch of the imagination and I had to learn through all of my mistakes. I clawed my way through university and gradually started building new businesses on the side and partnering up with my clients who had different skill sets. It wasn't all smooth sailing, in fact I failed in so many ventures along the way that I've lost count of how many failed businesses I've had.

I hustled hard to get into some private clinics in Harley Street and Wimpole Street as a behavioural therapist where I initially specialised in depression, but quickly branched into relationship therapy and then into business consultancy.

Over the next 15 years I mastered my craft. I read over 750 books in the area of psychology and business. I completed over 30,000 one to one sessions, helping people find what they wanted. I invested over £500,000 in my own education. I started well over 50 different businesses. Some worked, some were massive failures. I earned a lot of money and I also lost a lot. I made my first million by the age of 25 and it was then when I started documenting the process of why people get wealthy versus why people don't get wealthy. I started writing cases studies on my clients, studying successful people and adopting those habits and improving on them. I had the opportunity to win contracts with billionaires who turned over profits in the £20 billion plus zone. I worked closely with a Russian billionaire working with his company, providing a mentoring service to keep him on track. I lived with him for 4 years.

I kept on mastering my own skills and became completely obsessed with understanding the human mind and how to adapt it to get optimal results. This brings me up to the present moment where today, I am the owner of several different businesses that have profits in the 7 figure mark. I continue to upgrade my learning every step of the way. I have run events all over the world and have thousands of clients. I've impacted millions of people's lives to help them get what they want and where they want to be.

As a result I've been invited to speak alongside some great business people including Sir Alan Sugar and Gary Vaynerchuk and fill venues across London regularly, sharing some of the tools in this book.

Furthermore, the body of work I share with you today, is part of my PhD research. As I continue to push forward and create new ways of advanced thinking I'm passionate about helping people understand their mind and direct their focus so they can get what they want.

I'm very excited to share this with you and as I write this, I want you to know there really is nothing that special about me. I'm really a very basic person at heart, I promise you. However, what you'll discover from this book is very special and it's my pleasure to pass this gift onto you. I believe everyone can achieve anything they truly want, if they're willing to put the effort in, take the right guidance, get the right support, get the right education and most importantly, never give up on their dreams.

Thank you for your precious time, it means the world to me to know that you got this far. Remember that your time is your most important and precious asset that you'll ever have in life. Never waste it on anything or anyone that doesn't value your time.

When you have spent it, then it's gone. Value your time my friend, keep investing into yourself and honouring where you spend your time because the more you invest in yourself, the more valuable you become as an asset. Your greatest asset in the world is your mind because your mind will set you free, your mind will make you rich. Your mind will deliver everything you ever need. I know the road ahead may not be easy however, I want you to know, I'm always here for you. I'm never far away for those that seek, my door is always open for those that knock. My ears are always open for those that ask.

If you loved this book, please go over to Amazon and write a 5 star review so that others who read the book will also move further forward.

I look forward to meeting you one day. Maybe at a live event, come and say hi. I look forward to hearing your story.

Until then...

No matter what happens...

Never give up on your dreams!

I shall see you soon.

Big Love

Ed

Stay In Contact

www.edjcsmith.com - Come join a live webinar.

Breakthrough Success Summit - Get More From Your Life.

All social feeds just type Ed J C Smith and come say hi.

Facebook: Edjcsmith

Instagram: Edjcsmith

Youtube: Edjcsmith

Twitter: Edjcsmith

Linkedin: Edjcsmith

WHAT'S NEXT?

DO IT YOURSELF

I would strongly recommend you join my 49 day program called **THE 7 KEY ELEMENTS OF WEALTH** ™ to continue your growth and really hardwire everything you have learnt here.

If you want to join my online mentoring program then pop over to my site and invest in the next step, which comes with a 30-day money back Guarantee. If you are not completely blown away with the level of content that I provide, I will happily refund you your money, no questions asked. You will get a module everyday helping you further forward in the seven most important areas of your life so you can get the things you want.

All you have to do is go to **www.edjcsmith.com** join **THE 7 KEY ELEMENTS OF WEALTH** ™ live webinar and I will be excited as ever to continue with you and be a part of your journey. I have a special investment offer for you as a reader of this book, so be sure to snap up the special case study offer.

WORK WITH ME

If you would like me to hold you accountable personally, I have a range of options for you to choose from.

Send an email to my office **info@championacademy.co.uk** and my team of professional coaches will take you through the process, which includes completing a needs assessment form. They will also discuss other options that may be more affordable than having me as your exclusive mentor.

ACKNOWLEDGEMENTS

This goes out to my family. I love you. Each and everyone of you. You know who you are. I am going to personally deliver this book to you with your own special message. Without you this would not be possible. Family forever. Thank you for believing in me when I didn't.

Geraldine, Tina and Andy the most wonderful book team. I am so truly grateful for you.

To the 13 year old version of myself. We made it rain.

CELEBRITY ENDORSEMENTS

Gary Vaynerchuk **3 times Best Selling New York Times Author, TED Speaker, Owner of Vayner Media, Investor in Uber, Twitter & Snapchat**

"There is a reason that Ed is becoming the Number 1 in the UK today, because he gives more than anyone else. Ed is someone to watch out for, it won't be long until him and his academy are one of the best out there." **Gary Vaynerchuk** 3 times Best Selling New York Times Author, TED Speaker, Owner of Vayner Media, Investor in Uber, Twitter & Snapchat.

"There is a reason that Ed is becoming the Number 1 in the UK today, because he gives more than anyone else. Ed is someone to watch out for, it won't be long until him and his academy are one of the best out there."

Nick James **The UK's Largest Promoter, Author, Speaker Owner at Seriously Fun Business**

"In a world so full of hype and BS, it's rare to meet someone who is so successful, down to earth and also a genuinely nice guy (even if he is a bit cheesy). Ed is an extremely smart businessman and his agency are rock stars on all media. What he has taught us to reduce our costs in my business and how to generate clients has changed the way we run our business. If you are lucky enough to spend time with Ed he will help you dramatically increase your ability to earn more and contribute more."

Antony Stark **Property Developer Owner of Linea Homes Ltd**

"I came to Ed because I wanted to grow my business. 8 years later he is one of the most trusted people in my life. He has grown me as a person and the business is set to turnover £18.5 million this year. Without his help we would have never been able to do what we have done. Thank you Ed for all your help."

***Julianne Ponan* CEO - Creative Nature Virgin Start Up Key Note Speaker Youngest National Natwest Everywoman Artemis Award Winner The Guardian's Leader of the Year**

"I came to Ed because I wanted to grow my personal brand and there is no one better in the market to help you build your brand and business at the same time. His help has been priceless and with his help we were able to reach a much larger audience."

***Simon Coulson* UK's most successful marketing expert. Author, International Speaker Owner of Internet Business School**

"Ed is the real deal. Over my years of working with entrepreneurs he is someone that consistently delivers time and time again. If you want to take your business from 5 figures to 6 figures, or from 6 figures to 7 figures, then Ed will be able to rapidly transform your business and your life at the same time."

***Dr Melanie Lee* Chief Scientific Officer at BTG plc**

"I came to Ed because I needed help setting up my business. Over 10 years later now, we have been friends and business partners. There is no one I trust more and he has been instrumental in my life on a personal and professional level. I urge you to spend time with Ed as he will only bring out the best in you and empower you with all you truly need to be fulfilled and successful."

Richard Jones* Winner of *Britain's Got Talent

"I came to Ed because I was looking at new ways to stay ahead in the market and to build my brand whilst staying relevant in the market. Since spending time with Ed he has helped me in so many ways to develop my business and my personal brand and show me many ways to generate a greater income. Thank you Ed for your time. I recommend coming to his live events, they are absolutely fantastic and a must if you want to become more successful."

Eric Ho Author, Investor on Shark Tank International Speaker, Business Owner & Philanthropist

"Ed is one of the best out there. If you want to create more in your life and reach a balance of happiness at the same time, I urge you to spend time with him. What him and his team taught me around media management will change how you do everything. He is the number 1 in business today for getting more clients and making your business bullet proof."